"Dr. Courtney Paré's *Overcoming Relatio...* ...ne navigating the stormy seas of doubt ... ...a blend of empathetic writing and practi... ...ars and misconceptions that fuel relationship anxieties. Her approach is not just about coping but thriving. This book does more than just ease your mind; it equips you to build lasting, loving connections grounded in confidence and clarity. Essential reading for anyone looking to transform anxiety into a pathway for personal growth and deeper partnership."

—Jessica Baum, LMHC, author of
Anxiously Attached: Becoming More Secure in Life and Love

"Dr. Courtney Paré offers heartfelt wisdom for those who question how to approach developing a healthy relationship. In this day and age of growing anxiety, as both a healthcare and self-care issue, this book can be a beacon of light to many. It speaks powerfully to how to work with changes in both behavior and mindset that can lead to building a more stable inner foundation from which all relationships might flourish."

—Laurel Holland, author of *Courageous Woman* and *Live Your Inner Power*

"Offering deep and unique perspectives on relationship anxiety, *Overcoming Relationship Anxiety* provides a clear pathway for working out where you are in your relationship, where you want to be, and how you could begin to get there."

—Wayne J. Camara, PhD, Fellow, American Psychological Association and Association for Psychological Science

"Dr. Courtney Paré sheds a necessary and important spotlight on the hidden struggles of relationship anxiety and relationship OCD (ROCD). Through compassionate insights and actionable steps, her book empowers you to break free from this never-ending battle of doubt, fear, and uncertainty that can consume you. Courtney offers practical strategies and key takeaways that teach you everything you need to know on how to get out of this cycle and transform your doubt into confidence so that you can overcome your anxiety and build the secure, fulfilling relationship that you deserve."

—Haley Ostrow, LCSW

A Personal Approach to *Understanding Your Emotions*, *Building Your Self-Confidence*, and *Creating a Healthy, Secure Partnership*

OVERCOMING RELATIONSHIP ANXIETY

DR. COURTNEY PARÉ

ADAMS MEDIA
NEW YORK LONDON TORONTO SYDNEY NEW DELHI

Adams Media
An Imprint of Simon & Schuster, LLC
100 Technology Center Drive
Stoughton, Massachusetts 02072

First Adams Media trade paperback
edition December 2024

ADAMS MEDIA and colophon are
registered trademarks of Simon &
Schuster, LLC.

Simon & Schuster: Celebrating
100 Years of Publishing in 2024

For information about special discounts
for bulk purchases, please contact Simon
& Schuster Special Sales at 1-866-506-
1949 or business@simonandschuster.com.

The Simon & Schuster Speakers Bureau
can bring authors to your live event. For
more information or to book an event,
contact the Simon & Schuster Speakers
Bureau at 1-866-248-3049 or visit our
website at www.simonspeakers.com.

Interior design by Michelle Kelly

Manufactured in the
United States of America

1 2024

Library of Congress Cataloging-in-
Publication Data
Names: Paré, Courtney, author.
Title: Overcoming relationship anxiety /
Dr. Courtney Paré.
Description: Stoughton, Massachusetts:
Adams Media, [2024] | Includes
bibliographical references and index.
Identifiers: LCCN 2024038274 |
ISBN 9781507222683 (pb) | ISBN
9781507222690 (ebook)
Subjects: LCSH: Interpersonal relations. |
Anxiety. | Self-confidence.
Classification: LCC HM1106 .P362 2024
| DDC 302--dc23/eng/20240904
LC record available at https://lccn.loc.gov/
2024038274

ISBN 978-1-5072-2268-3
ISBN 978-1-5072-2269-0 (ebook)

DEDICATION

In loving memory of my best friend, Rondo. I started this book with you by my side and finished it holding you in my heart, where you'll forever stay. I love you.

And, to Monroe. You've been a light in my life since the day you were born. May you always find your confidence, courage, and values as you navigate the many relationships that await you. I love you.

CONTENTS

ACKNOWLEDGMENTS

Writing a book was always a distant dream, something I might pursue "someday." That "someday" came more quickly and unexpectedly than I imagined when Julia Belkas approached me with the opportunity to write this book. Julia, thank you for believing in me and the potential of this book from day one. It wouldn't exist without you.

I'm grateful to my editing team for their help in shaping this book into what it is today, especially Laura Daly. Your valuable suggestions and support throughout the process, as well as your encouragement during my moments of doubt and anxiety, were invaluable.

I'd like to thank the entire Adams Media team for your dedication and patience in bringing this book to life. Your understanding throughout this process has been deeply appreciated.

Laurel, your unwavering confidence in me and this book from start to finish was incredibly supportive. Your guidance and encouragement were instrumental in completing this project. Thank you for believing in me.

Mark, thank you for listening to and supporting me through the myriad of emotions that came up during this project. I am deeply grateful for your time, patience, and friendship.

Komal, thank you for promptly providing feedback on short notice. Both your perspective and encouragement contributed to my confidence and motivation to keep going. I appreciate you.

Wendy, Justin, and Harleen, your enthusiasm and encouragement in my writing this book did not go unnoticed and are much appreciated.

Mom and Dad, thank you for the countless hours you each spent with me on the phone during my deepest grief. Your support created the space I needed to begin processing my loss and return to writing. You are two of the most impactful relationships in my life, and I am grateful for every opportunity we get to enjoy, heal, and strengthen our individual relationships. I love you both.

To my first and longest-standing relationships, my siblings—Ashley, Jarred, Robin, and Nina. We've shared many of life's joys and challenges, and I've learned so much about myself and relationships from each of you. I cherish the special childhood memories we've created and love that we continue to make fun and meaningful memories into adulthood. I love you all and deeply value our relationships.

Templeton, Figaro, and Rondo, you are, and forever will be, woven into everything I do. The happiest parts of me are made up of you. You will always be a part of my heart.

Lastly, I'd like to thank my clients. Witnessing your courage, vulnerability, and determination has profoundly influenced the writing of this book. Your willingness to open your hearts and minds, and trust me to walk alongside you on your healing journey, is something I do not take for granted. From the struggles to the triumphs, I learn from and am inspired by each of you every day.

INTRODUCTION

In my early twenties, I had an amazing partner—thoughtful, loving, patient, supportive, and funny. Of course, every moment we shared together wasn't perfect, but overall our relationship was great...and yet I couldn't shake the feeling that it might not be good enough. I questioned so many things: Did he really love me? Would he leave me? Is there someone else out there who might be an even better fit for me? My heart was in the relationship, but my mind was in a spiral of doubt and insecurity. We eventually drifted apart, and I often wonder if things would've turned out differently if I had the knowledge I have today.

While I'll never know the answer to that, I do know that the uncertainty, anxiety, and doubt I experienced in my relationship is something many other people are also experiencing. No matter how amazing their partner, they question their relationship and are plagued by uncertainty and indecision. They wonder if it's right, if they're enough, if they're truly loved, or if they might be settling for less than their soulmate.

If this situation sounds familiar, know you are not alone. I've been there myself and come out the other side. I've since used my expertise as a holistic anxiety coach to guide countless others through the web of emotions that accompanies relationship anxiety, and this book is designed to support you in breaking free from the grip of anxiety as well. Whether you're currently in a relationship, desiring a relationship, or have a history of avoiding or sabotaging relationships, I'll offer you valuable information and suggestions that can help you feel calmer and more secure.

Drawing from my own experience with relationship anxiety, my education, and my clinical practice, this book paves the way for you to go from feeling constantly unsure and unsettled in your relationship to feeling confident, content, and connected to your partner. While reading this book will not give you certainty around the "rightness" of your relationship, it will give you something even better: the ability to truly thrive in your relationship without needing that certainty. You'll also learn how to find your own personalized path to healing based on your experiences instead of searching for a simple, one-size-fits-all solution.

This book is divided into two parts. Part 1: Understanding Relationship Anxiety delves into anxiety's origins, manifestations, and the reasons you might be trapped in an anxiety cycle. Part 2: Navigating Relationship Anxiety equips you with the skills and support needed to help you better identify your relationship vision and values, take control where you can, and thrive despite uncertainty. When you do that, you'll enjoy deeper intimacy and create a deeply connected relationship that you're actually excited—and not afraid—to commit to.

Navigating a relationship is challenging. Navigating a relationship while experiencing anxiety is even more challenging, but it can be done! Learning to be relational is a skill. Learning to trust yourself and your partner is a skill. Learning to tolerate waves of discomfort and disappointment is a skill. It makes sense you're struggling to do those things; you probably weren't ever taught how. The good news is, skills can be learned! *Overcoming Relationship Anxiety* will teach you powerful ways to manage the complexities of relationships with more ease and less anxiety.

Please note that the information shared throughout this book applies to individuals who are experiencing anxiety in otherwise healthy relationships. The content, strategies, and exercises covered may not be supportive for those who are in toxic or abusive relationships. Please seek professional help if you are in an abusive situation. Also, while relationship anxiety can occur in any relationship, this book focuses specifically on monogamous romantic relationships.

OVERCOMING RELATIONSHIP ANXIETY

UNDERSTANDING RELATIONSHIP ANXIETY

Welcome to Part 1 of *Overcoming Relationship Anxiety*, which will explore what relationship anxiety is, its underlying causes, how it could be manifesting in your relationship, and the myths and behaviors that could be contributing to keeping you stuck in an anxious cycle. Anxiety is complicated and multifaceted, but you will learn to recognize signs that it's at work in your relationship. You'll also explore how anxiety might be showing up in your relationship—both physically and emotionally—and examine various factors that can contribute to its onset and exacerbations.

This part will also identify and challenge the myths and illusions that relationship anxiety often perpetuates. From the notion of finding "The One" to the fear of settling for less, you will confront societal expectations and explore more realistic perspectives on love and partnership. Once you see through these myths, you'll begin to feel more hopeful and empowered to overcome your anxiety.

Lastly, you will examine the behaviors that can keep you stuck in a cycle of anxiety. Whether it's seeking continuous reassurance, engaging in avoidance tactics, or succumbing to the urge to test or confess to your partner, you'll uncover what is motivating these behaviors and discover practical strategies to shift into new and healthier patterns.

Throughout Part 1, you will be reminded of two important things: Anxiety is not your fault, and it does not have to be a life sentence. The goal of this part is to empower you with knowledge, insight, and tools to more deeply understand your anxiety, setting the foundation to overcome it. When you gain a deeper understanding of the roots of anxiety, start recognizing its lies, and practice exercises to better navigate its challenges, you can begin to release doubt, embrace confidence, and build more peaceful and fulfilling relationships.

CHAPTER 1

WHAT IS RELATIONSHIP ANXIETY?

There it is again—the tug to type "how do I know if I'm in love" into the search bar. A part of you knows it's just a silly search that's never going to actually answer your question, while another part of you is still hoping it will. This might be such a habit for you that you've already read most of the articles that pop up, completed all the quizzes, and searched all the discussion boards. And yet, that doesn't stop you from clicking a link that promises answers: "Is Your Partner 'The One'? Take the quiz to find out if you're dating your soulmate." Anxiously awaiting your relationship fate, you click through the questions and let out a huge sigh of relief when your results land on "They're definitely 'The One.' You two are a perfect match." You feel better…for now.

If that scenario sounds familiar, you're in good company. Relationships are treasures, teachers…and triggers. They're often one of our greatest sources of joy, pleasure, support, and fulfillment. Unfortunately, for some, they can also be a source of great stress, uncertainty, and anxiety. In this chapter, you will learn how experiencing doubt and conflicting feelings could be a result of living with relationship anxiety. Let's dive into learning what relationship anxiety is and why you could be experiencing it, what's happening within your brain and body when you're in the thick of an anxiety spiral, and, most importantly, how you can begin to overcome it.

EVERYBODY FEELS DOUBT

Choosing to be in a partnership is a big deal, so it's no wonder you feel pressure to make the "right" decision. Navigating relationships might even feel like you're in a tug-of-war between opening your heart and guarding your vulnerabilities. It makes sense that you'd put a lot of thought into who you're sharing your time, your heart, and possibly, your *life* with. That's why you might find your mind filled with questions like:

- Are we compatible enough?
- Would they stay with me if something serious happened?
- Do we miss one another enough when we're apart?
- Are they funny enough? Romantic enough? Spontaneous enough?
- Do my friends think they're boring? Do their friends think I'm boring?
- What if they cheat on me? What if *I* cheat on *them*?
- Do they really love me? Do I really love them?
- Would I be having these doubts if they were "The One"?

Questioning your relationship is common. Everyone—yes, even those who seem to have the picture-perfect relationship—experiences relationship doubt and anxiety. After all…

- It's natural, and healthy, to question your relationship from time to time.
- It's reasonable to assess compatibility and shared values in the beginning of a relationship.
- It's understandable to reflect and reassess before major milestones, such as becoming exclusive, meeting your significant other's family and friends, moving in together, adopting a pet, getting engaged, having children, etc.
- It's natural to want to be reassured that your partner loves and values you.

But how much doubt is *too much*? When your doubts, questions, and worries become a constant narrative rather than an occasional blip on the radar, that's a clear sign your relationship anxiety needs attention.

> Case Study: Wrestling with Uncertainty

Aubrey was having coffee with her partner, Devin. They had a great relationship, but as she looked over at him that morning, Aubrey suddenly had a moment of panic and thought, "Do I *really* love him? Have I just been pretending? Do I feel anything for him at all? Should we even be together?" Aubrey quickly got quiet and distant as she wrestled with the uncertainty in her head. Feelings of joy and relaxation were quickly replaced with feelings of doubt and anxiety.

This wasn't a new occurrence for Aubrey. While things with Devin seemed to be going well overall, she continuously doubted her feelings and questioned their connection and compatibility. Perhaps you can relate to Aubrey—do you have a nagging feeling that something is not quite right, but you can't put your finger on exactly what's wrong? Your heart tells you your relationship is great, while your mind questions, "But what if it isn't!?" This exhausting exchange between your heart and your mind may preoccupy so much of your time and energy that it overshadows all other aspects of your relationship. If you're feeling this way, you're definitely not alone! Keep reading for more information and suggestions about how to work through these thoughts.

WHAT IS RELATIONSHIP ANXIETY?

We all want to be loved. In fact, feeling loved is one of the most fundamental human needs. And while we can experience love in many forms, the overwhelming majority of us desire deep, lasting love with a romantic partner. A 2022 survey that interviewed nearly two thousand US adults concluded that 94 percent of women and 88 percent of men believe in "true love." So we're all on the same page—but why then, when we desire to be in partnership, do we find ourselves filled with doubt and confusion rather than peace and optimism when we're finally in one? This might be due to an experience known as relationship anxiety.

Relationship anxiety might be a term that's new to you or one you're intimately familiar with. For the context of this book, relationship anxiety refers to a preoccupation with the "rightness" of your relationship. It's characterized by a general persistence of doubt, insecurity, and worry surrounding your relationship without significant evidence to support that worry. There is an underlying fear that no matter how well the relationship seems to be going, it's only a matter of time before it will take a turn for the worse. This doubt and fear are time-consuming, distressing, and in opposition to the way you truly feel toward your partner.

Common Signs of Relationship Anxiety

Relationship anxiety can show up in a number of different ways. Let's look at some of the most common.

- **Doubting your partner's feelings for you (or yours for them):** You're unsure if you really matter to your partner and frequently question their love and commitment, even when there's no apparent reason to doubt their feelings. You might also be unsure if you really care about your partner, even when you know you do.
- **Questioning your compatibility:** You find yourself caught up in minute details, such as whether or not you like the same music, movies, and sports teams while overlooking the more meaningful areas where you are compatible.
- **Overanalyzing:** You dissect every text message or conversation and hyperfocus on facial expression, body language, and tone of voice, searching for hidden meanings or signs of potential trouble.

- **Assessing attractiveness:** You question if you find your partner attractive and/or wonder if they're really attracted to you. You worry they're interested in sex too often or not enough. You might find yourself fixated on your partner's "flaws," such as the size of their nose, length of their hair, fashion choices, or the way they chew their food.

- **Engaging in perfectionism:** You place unrealistic expectations on yourself to be the perfect partner, fearing that a mistake or perceived flaw could lead to the end of the relationship. Similarly, you might place expectations on your partner to be perfect, and you judge their lack of perfection as "evidence" that you should end the relationship.

- **Partner pleasing:** Your anxiety could lead you to avoid expressing your needs, desires, or opinions. You'll go to great lengths to tamp down conflict or disagreements, even if that means suppressing your needs and concerns out of fear they'll judge you or leave you.

- **Catastrophizing:** You tend to imagine worst-case scenarios and constantly feel on edge, thinking it's only a matter of time before the other shoe will drop.

- **Experiencing an emotional rollercoaster:** Your emotions can feel like they're on a wild ride, rapidly shifting from confidence and contentment to anxiety and uncertainty, depending on whichever story your mind conjures up in the moment.

- **Experiencing jealousy and possessiveness:** You might experience jealousy, possessiveness, or insecurity when your partner interacts with others, even in platonic settings. You might attempt to control who your partner interacts with and how they spend their time. You might even try to make your partner jealous, interpreting their jealousy as confirmation of their love for you.

- **Feeling physical discomfort:** You might notice chronic or intermittent headaches, stomachaches, sleep disturbances, appetite changes, and/or muscle tension.

You may not experience all of these habits or thinking patterns, but if many of them resonate with you, it's likely that anxiety is interfering with your relationship.

CONTRIBUTING FACTORS

While there isn't always an identifiable cause, there are a variety of factors that might put you at greater risk of experiencing anxiety in your relationship. Some of these factors include:

Chronic Stress

Being exposed to frequent or prolonged stress can put you into "survival mode." Living in this keyed up state can cause you to feel worried and uncertain about everything, including your relationship.

Low Self-Worth

Feeling as though you are undeserving of the things you want in life can put you at odds with creating a healthy, fulfilling partnership. Putting yourself down or believing that you are unworthy or unlovable can make it difficult for you to trust your partner's love and commitment. These self-limiting beliefs might lead you to subconsciously engage in behaviors that push your partner away in order to confirm the belief that you are unworthy.

Difficult Experiences in Early Childhood

Our early childhood experiences play an integral role in shaping our beliefs, personality, attachment style, and self-esteem. Witnessing the relationships of your caregivers and/or elders provided you with your earliest examples and expectations of relationships. According to data provided by the US Centers for Disease Control and Prevention, roughly 64 percent of US adults reported experiencing at least one "adverse childhood experience" (which could include suffering physical, sexual, and/or emotional abuse; witnessing domestic violence; facing racism or discrimination; etc.) and about 17 percent reported experiencing four or more. Experiencing these can lead to nervous system dysregulation, a decrease in your ability to cope with stressful situations, and a potential increase in your risk of developing an anxiety disorder.

Previous Relationship Experiences

The lens through which you view your current or future relationships can be influenced by your previous relationship experiences. Understandably, if a past partner cheated on you, broke things off unexpectedly, or abandoned, betrayed, or misled you, you might have trouble trusting in a relationship again.

However, it's not just relationships that end "badly" that can lead to relationship anxiety. Sometimes, it's the relationships that end on good terms or those in which you simply grow apart that can cause the most anxiety. These types of relationships might lead you to doubt if another relationship could stack up if this "good one" didn't, if any relationship can last, and if it's worth it to open your heart again.

History of Trauma

Traumatic experiences change how you view, interpret, and interact with the world around you. Both physical and emotional traumas can have significant and lasting effects on your nervous system and your ability to cope with conflict, disappointment, uncertainty, and physical and emotional intimacy. What is considered traumatic is highly individualized as it is less about the event itself and more about how the event affected the individual. However, some common traumatic experiences could include:

- Experiencing or witnessing physical, sexual, or emotional abuse.
- Experiencing emotional neglect (being ignored or isolated, denied affection, humiliated, etc.) or physical neglect (lack of basic needs, such as shelter, clothing, food, medical care, etc.).

- Being exposed to substance use or abuse.
- Experiencing the traumatic loss of a loved one.
- Experiencing an accident or major injury.
- Witnessing or surviving natural disasters.

Please note that while the concepts and skills in this book are designed to be supportive to anyone, if you have a history of unprocessed trauma, you might benefit from working with a trained professional to process your trauma prior to working through this book. It's also okay to skip over chapters or exercises and come back to them as you feel ready to do so.

Lack of Healthy Role Models

If you do not (or did not) have examples of healthy, loving, and secure partnerships, it can be challenging to believe that this type of relationship could be possible for you. Since the brain prefers what is familiar, pursuing a type of partnership that is unfamiliar to you (even if it's a good type!) could leave you feeling guarded, distant, or doubtful.

Similarly, if you do not (or did not) have examples of individuals healthily expressing emotions, handling conflict, and tolerating moments of discomfort, you might not have developed the skills and confidence necessary to navigate these circumstances in your own life.

Genetics

A variety of studies show that the presence of anxiety can be influenced by genetic factors. While there is no single "anxiety gene," it is frequently observed that anxiety disorders run in families. It's estimated that 30–40 percent of this heritability could be due to biological/genetic factors. However, it's important to note that genetic, environmental, and parenting style factors combined play a significant role in whether or not an anxiety disorder will be "passed down" to a child.

Lifestyle

The way you eat, drink, move, rest, speak, and play can impact your body physiologically and psychologically. These factors can influence your ability, or lack thereof, to tolerate discomfort and cope with stressful situations.

Underlying Health Conditions

Certain nutrient deficiencies, hormonal imbalances, autoimmune conditions, and chronic illnesses might increase symptoms of anxiety and/or lead to nervous system dysregulation.

Presence of Other Mental Health Disorders

While you do not have to have a diagnosed mental health disorder to experience relationship anxiety, living with a mental health disorder such as generalized anxiety disorder (GAD), social anxiety disorder (SAD), obsessive-compulsive disorder (OCD), post-traumatic stress disorder (PTSD), premenstrual dysphoric disorder (PMDD), or borderline personality disorder (BPD), to name a few, could make you more susceptible to experiencing anxiety, doubt, and insecurity surrounding your relationship.

If one or more of these criteria spoke to your situation, please know that progress is still possible. These factors could help explain where your journey with anxiety began, but they do not dictate where it will end. One of the most incredible gifts of being human is that each of us has the power to unlearn old patterns and stories, retrain our brain to respond in a new way, heal our nervous system, and show up to ourselves and our relationships with newfound confidence and clarity. You are no exception, and choosing to pick up this book indicates that you are already on your way there!

Relationship Anxiety Is Not a Personal Weakness

If you were nodding along with one or more examples or contributing factors just listed, it does not mean there is something wrong with you—or your relationship! Experiencing relationship anxiety is not a personal weakness or an indicator that your relationship is doomed. In fact, it could actually be a sign that you're a deeply caring person who values your partner and doesn't want to lose them, hurt them, or be hurt by them. Remember, *all* relationships have moments of doubt and insecurity. While insecurity is a shared human experience, if you find yourself worrying about your relationship more often than you are enjoying your relationship, this book will help you manage and rightsize your feelings.

WHAT PURPOSE DOES ANXIETY SERVE, ANYWAY?

Before we start managing those anxious feelings, though, let's first take a moment to understand why they exist in the first place. As long as humans have existed, so too have feelings of fear and anxiety. They're part of our nervous system, which is an internal alarm system that is always evaluating our surroundings for potential threats. When danger is detected, various parts of our brain kick into gear. These include rational, emotional, and instinctive components, all working together to ensure we avoid harm. This coordinated effort is known as the fight-or-flight response (also referred to as the fight-flight-freeze-fawn response).

This instinctive stress response triggers rapid hormonal and physiological changes geared toward ensuring your survival. If you're ever in the unfortunate situation of being chased by a bear in the woods, this response is what would activate! While crucial when facing a literal bear in the woods, what about when the fight-or-flight response gets triggered by less critical concerns, like your crush taking longer to respond to a text or your partner being in a grumpy mood on vacation?

That's when you enter nervous system dysregulation, which can contribute to relationship anxiety.

SYMPTOMS OF CHRONIC STRESS

We've all felt short-term stress before—but chronic stress can show up in different ways. Following are some of the many physical and emotional symptoms that could result from the acute and/or chronic activation of the stress response. Perhaps you've noticed some of these regularly showing up in your own life.

Physical Symptoms
- Increased heart rate
- Visual disturbances
- Difficulty swallowing
- Digestive distress
- Changes in appetite
- Jaw clenching
- Changes in libido
- Dizziness/brain fog
- Sleep disturbances
- Headaches
- Numbness and tingling in extremities
- Muscle tension
- Restlessness

Emotional or Thought-Based Symptoms
- Fear/anxiety
- Racing thoughts
- Difficulty concentrating
- Thinking of worst-case scenarios (catastrophizing)
- Guilt

- Hyperfixation/preoccupation
- Feeling irritable or on edge
- Insecurity
- Helplessness
- Feelings of dread or impending doom
- Feeling like you're "going crazy" or "losing your mind"
- Mood swings
- Loneliness/withdrawal

If you've been experiencing any of these symptoms, you might be familiar with the overwhelming sensation that, in this activated state, the world can suddenly seem like a dangerous place. This is because your perception of everything—from how you see and hear things to how you think and breathe—is filtered through a lens of fear. It can seem like everything and everyone is against you. The intention here is, of course, that your body is trying to protect you, but in the absence of a true threat, it can certainly feel like your brain is doing you more harm than good.

WHEN YOU'RE IN SURVIVAL MODE TOO OFTEN

Your body is designed to switch between the sympathetic (fight-or-flight) and parasympathetic (rest-and-digest) nervous system states. Ideally, the stress response activates the sympathetic system briefly to help you survive a perceived threat and then you return to a state of calm—the fancy name for that is *parasympathetic homeostasis*. However, for many people today, this alarm system seems to be overworking, misfiring, or staying activated for too long, putting you in a prolonged period of "survival mode." This means you're experiencing nervous system dysregulation.

Sensing Danger

Survival mode is supposed to be a short-term situation. When you're *living* in survival mode, your body is not feeling safe a large part of the time. Feeling content and connected to your partner is nearly impossible when you sense danger. It's understandable that you'd be hesitant; in this primed-for-survival, activated state, your brain could be mistaking your partner as the threat, regardless of how loving and supportive they may be. Think of it as your rational, thinking brain going offline and your instinctive brain taking over. The instinctive part of your brain isn't interested in the lovely dinner date the two of you shared last weekend; it's only interested in assessing your partner's tone of voice, body language, and intentions at the present moment.

Through this "survival lens," you can easily get a skewed view of your partner, which can be confusing and make you doubt yourself. Two days ago, you felt happily in love, safe in their arms, and today you're unsure if you feel anything positive toward them at all. It can be especially difficult to trust yourself, never mind your partner, when your body is sending you these types of mixed signals.

Learning that some of the doubt, anxiety, and hypervigilance you feel surrounding your relationship could be a result of a dysregulated nervous system might feel overwhelming, but simply being aware of this situation is the first step to overcoming it. Gaining insight into the roots of your anxiety empowers you to take control of your healing journey.

RELATIONSHIP ANXIETY VS. RELATIONSHIP OCD

Relationship anxiety and relationship obsessive-compulsive disorder (ROCD) are distinct but closely related challenges. Relationship anxiety might stem from a general fear of rejection, abandonment, or vulnerability and prompts an internal dialogue questioning compatibility, commitment, and love.

In contrast, ROCD is a specific subtype of obsessive-compulsive disorder (OCD) characterized by intrusive, distressing thoughts about the relationship, leading to ritualistic behaviors aimed at neutralizing anxiety and gaining certainty. To receive an OCD diagnosis, specific criteria must be met. These criteria include the presence of both obsessions and compulsions. These symptoms cause significant distress and functional impairment, and they are present on most days.

Relationship anxiety varies in severity and can exist on a spectrum, whereas ROCD tends to be more persistent and severe. While not always the case, experiencing ROCD is usually less about someone feeling insecure about their partner's feelings toward them, and more about their wanting to feel certain their partner and relationship are "right." Anyone with ROCD likely has relationship anxiety, but not everyone with relationship anxiety has ROCD.

While both relationship anxiety and ROCD present with doubt around a relationship, it's important to note that these persistent feelings of anxiety are not reflective of the partner an individual is with. Much to the dismay of those impacted, these challenges persist no matter how loving and supportive their partner is.

Whether you find yourself meeting the diagnostic criteria or not, both experiences deserve understanding and support. In the upcoming chapters, you'll learn tools and concepts that can benefit anyone facing relationship challenges, regardless of where you fall on the severity spectrum. If you want more personalized information, consider reaching out to a licensed professional trained in relationship anxiety and OCD or refer to the International OCD Foundation's website shown in the Resource List at the back of this book for additional guidance. There is support available for your unique journey.

OVERCOMING RELATIONSHIP ANXIETY

LEARN TO EMBRACE DISCOMFORT

A key component to having a healthier relationship with your *partner* is first beginning to have a healthier relationship with your *anxiety.* While it might not always feel like it, your body (including your anxiety) is always on your side. However, just because you're feeling anxious does not mean there is a threat, and just because you're feeling uncomfortable does not mean you're in danger.

While it's natural to want to run away from danger, a cornerstone of anxiety healing is to be willing to "sit with," or tolerate, some discomfort. Despite how intense the discomfort might feel in the moment, it's important to remember that discomfort does not necessarily equal danger. Accepting—rather than avoiding—discomfort within your relationship is a foundational skill when overcoming relationship anxiety and building a confident partnership.

Confirmation Bias Can Make New Skills Hard to Learn

Why can implementing new skills be so difficult even when you know you're tired of doing things the old way? Because your brain has been operating for years, perhaps even decades, under its current belief system...that's a lot of time to accumulate experiences, expectations, and evidence to support what it currently (mostly subconsciously) believes. What you believe affects how you see things, and that affects how you act, including how you interact with your partner. This is due in large part to a phenomenon known as confirmation bias. A term coined by psychologist Peter Wason, PhD, *confirmation bias* refers to the tendency to notice, collect, evaluate, and emphasize evidence in a way that supports your existing beliefs. This bias leads you to dismiss evidence to the contrary, even if it goes against your best interests or desires.

In the upcoming chapters, you will learn how to begin leaning toward discomfort and uncertainty rather than away from it. If the idea of handling discomfort feels tough...you're right, it really can be. But you can do it! We all prefer comfort in our daily lives. From changing into our most comfy clothes the moment we walk in the door, to choosing the most comfortable chair or spot on the couch, to eating comfort foods and binging on comfort shows, it's natural to prefer to be as comfortable as we can! Considering this, actively looking for discomfort might feel challenging. Learning to tolerate discomfort is one of the many skills throughout this book that may not come naturally.

If you're feeling discouraged as you begin to practice this skill—or any of the upcoming skills in this book—here are two things to keep in mind:

- **It's challenging because it's new:** Your brain prefers to be right and likes predictability, so change—even positive change—can feel wrong at first. Remind yourself that you're new at it, not bad at it. It feels uncomfortable not because it's *wrong* but because it's *different* than what you're used to.
- **You're capable of handling a challenge:** You're likely far more capable than you're giving yourself credit for. Just look at how far you've come already. Living with the weight of relationship anxiety is challenging, and you're still here, learning to overcome it. You can do this!

You can even use these two statements as positive reminders that you repeat to yourself, either aloud or silently, as you learn and practice these new skills.

Exercise:
Regulating Your Nervous System

Try dedicating a few minutes each day to doing exercises that help you regulate your nervous system in order to decrease symptoms of anxiety and increase your willingness to incorporate new patterns of thought and behavior. Following are some tools and strategies to help you get started. Do your best to pick one or two and commit to utilizing them daily for at least thirty days.

- **Vagus nerve stimulation:** Singing, humming, gargling, or gently massaging the area behind your ear lobe can help increase vagal tone, which leads to a higher capacity to handle stress, change, and discomfort.
- **Cold plunge or cold face splash:** Immersing your face or body in cold water for thirty seconds to two minutes can help reset your nervous system, decrease the stress hormone cortisol, and increase the "feel good" neurotransmitter dopamine.
- **Binaural beats:** Listening through headphones to two slightly different frequencies at the same time creates an auditory phenomenon known as binaural beats, which can help synchronize your brain hemispheres and promote balance and calm.
- **Emotional Freedom Technique (EFT):** Tapping on specific meridian points such as above your eyebrow or under your nose can help disrupt the fight-or-flight response and offer your body a pathway for emotional release.
- **Alternate Nostril Breathing (Nadi Shodhana):** This is a yogic breathing technique that involves gently closing one nostril at a time while inhaling and exhaling. It helps balance the nervous system and reduce anxiety.
- **Acupuncture:** Acupuncture, a component of Traditional Chinese Medicine (TCM) in which thin needles are inserted into the body, might promote energy flow and balance within the nervous system.
- **Herbal medicine:** Herbs such as fresh milky oat (*Avena sativa*), holy basil (*Ocimum tenuiflorum*), hops (*Humulus lupulus*), and lemon balm (*Melissa officinalis*) have traditionally been used to nourish the nervous system. Consuming them in tea or tincture form can also be a soothing ritual.

Note: Always check with your healthcare provider before starting or stopping any herbal treatments, supplements, or healing techniques.

Key Takeaways

- Everyone will have moments of doubt and uncertainty in relationships. However, relationship anxiety goes beyond occasional doubts and is marked by persistent feelings of insecurity and worry, often without clear justification.
- Relationship anxiety can stem from various factors, including a chronically activated sympathetic nervous system. Learning to regulate your nervous system through different techniques can help alleviate some anxiety symptoms and foster a sense of safety.
- Relationship anxiety varies in intensity, and everyone experiences it differently. Regardless of where you fall on the spectrum, embracing discomfort, tolerating uncertainty, and building confidence are valuable steps toward managing and overcoming it.

CHAPTER 2

CHALLENGING THE MYTHS AND LIES RELATIONSHIP ANXIETY TELLS YOU

It's not your fault—you've been misled. Your anxiety, though it has the best intentions, has been telling you some deceptive stories. Stories of endless passion, constant attraction, and, of course, a promise that when you know, you know. You're probably thinking, "That is the problem; I *don't* know!" You're not alone in feeling this way. In fact, *no one* has 100 percent certainty regarding their relationships. To the hopeless romantic's dismay, no one is guaranteed a "happily ever after." The good news is, despite what your anxiety may have you believing, you do *not* need certainty, nor the promise of a happily ever after, to have a wonderful partnership and fulfilling life.

Many times, people have a hard time seeing their own happiness because they're stuck in a comparison trap. When the world bombards you with movies, novels, images, and stories depicting fiery and effortless love, it's easy to wonder why your relationship doesn't match up. Of course, these are all common myths and lies that relationship anxiety might lead you to believe. In this chapter, we'll expose these misconceptions, and you'll discover that true relationship freedom doesn't come from finding the "perfect partner"—it comes from understanding there is no such thing as a perfect partner.

MYTH NUMBER ONE:
TRUE LOVE FEELS LIKE A FAIRY TALE

Myth: When you meet the right person, you'll fall in love at first sight and live happily ever after. Love will come easily, romance will be constant, and life will feel complete.

Fact: Real-life love is a continuous dance between joy and challenge, harmony and disharmony. It might look different than fairy-tale love, but it can be just as meaningful and magical when it's built through embracing your unique and imperfect shared experiences.

Many of us search for a love story akin to a fairy tale, filled with endless passion and undeniable destiny. This is understandable, since a powerful "nothing will stop us from being together" love story is unforgettable. We all know the classic stories that end with a ride off into the sunset—the blockbuster movies that drive home the notion of "fate" and the captivating novels that evoke deep emotions.

While there is nothing wrong with indulging in a good rom-com or fairy tale, when you become so emotionally invested that you forget these are well-told *stories*, you can begin to have a skewed view of what being in love really looks and feels like.

The Reality: Everyone Is Human, and Life Just Isn't That Exciting

Let's face it: Real-life love doesn't typically follow a Hollywood script. The reality of human partnership is far more nuanced, and frankly much less exciting, than any made-for-entertainment narrative portrays.

Even though your love life probably isn't unfolding like a movie script, it doesn't mean there is something wrong with you or your relationship! With the rise of "reality" TV, it's easy to mistake scripted and edited drama for genuine human connection. While it's true that the media shapes our beliefs about gender roles, cultural norms, sex, intimacy, and more, it's crucial to recognize that these narratives are tailored for entertainment, not as blueprints for our relationships.

Healthy relationships aren't a constant whirlwind of passion, conflict, and drama. They also do not follow a linear path of meeting, falling in love, resolving one hiccup pretty easily, and then riding off into the sunset. They're instead a daily mix of connection, disconnection, and mundane moments that a solid foundation of love is built from over time. While the daily ups and downs of a healthy love story might lack the intensity of a blockbuster, they provide the stability necessary for a secure and confident relationship.

Look for a More Realistic Fairy Tale

If you're a hopeless romantic, all is not lost! You still can have your fairy tale; it will just look different from the stories you read as a child or the movies you loved as a teen. It's unlikely you'll end up randomly spilling your cup of coffee on your soulmate, who happens to be in town from across the world renovating their grandmother's mansion. The truth is this: Movies wouldn't be box office hits, romance novels wouldn't be bestsellers, and reality TV wouldn't get high ratings if they chose to tell an ordinary love story. And yet, those "ordinary" stories are exactly what will bring you the peace you're looking for in partnership, if you're willing to allow it in.

While you won't have to sell your soul to prove your love, creating your own modern-day fairy tale may demand something even scarier—vulnerability and self-trust. You want your journey to actively build love—not passively stumble upon it—even in the face of discomfort and uncertainty.

Meet Cutes Don't Predetermine Your Love Story

Actively building love often means giving relationships some time to develop. One of the most appealing parts of an iconic love story is the notion of romantic destiny—from the get-go, it was meant to be. In other words, the "meet cute." A meet cute is an encounter, typically a scene in a movie, novel, or TV show, where two people meet for the first time in an amusing or a serendipitous way and go on to develop a romantic relationship. When you're struggling with relationship anxiety, this expectation could influence you in a handful of ways, including:

- Attempting to force or manipulate "coincidental" encounters with potential partners
- Staying in an uninspiring or toxic relationship because of the serendipitous way it started out
- Avoiding opportunities that might lead you to meet someone in a "boring" way
- Not pursuing—or prematurely calling off—a potentially meaningful relationship because it didn't have an exciting start

While the "How did you two meet?" question is almost unavoidable if you're in a relationship, how you answer it truly doesn't matter. Whether it started out Disney's *101 Dalmatians*–style, with the two of you tangled up in your dog's leash at the dog park, or it began with a "hey" on a dating app is insignificant to the quality and longevity of your relationship. Sure, the dog park makes for a better *story*, but the way you and your partner *live* is far more significant than the way you *met*.

How you meet your partner doesn't predetermine your love story. Seemingly uneventful meetings can blossom into successful and fulfilling relationships, while the most charming of encounters may lead to unexpected challenges. Know that within a healthy partnership, there will be plenty of time to create special memories together and collect cute stories to share. There's no need to force a meet cute or to feel bad about how you met your partner.

MYTH NUMBER TWO: THE EXISTENCE OF "THE ONE"

Myth: There is only one person out there you could create a meaningful, connected, and fulfilling relationship with, and you will instantaneously know who they are when you meet them.

Fact: There are multiple "special someones" out there you could create a meaningful, connected, and fulfilling relationship with, and you learn who these people are (and are not) through shared experiences over time.

Emerging from the expectations set by fairy tales is the concept of "The One." You could think of this like a relationship unicorn. In a romantic sense, "The One" describes the single other human being on planet Earth you could have the best and most successful partnership with—the one who completes you. Believing in the existence of "The One" implies that there is a best person out there for you and that if/when you find this person, all your needs will be satisfied, doubts will subside, and you'll feel whole. Who wouldn't want that!?

The problem is the flip side: If you *do not* find this person, it suggests you might miss out on ever experiencing "true love." Needless to say, the quest to find "The One" can be pressure filled and anxiety producing. With societal promises of instant chemistry and easy love, it's understandable that you would feel pressure to search endlessly for this unicorn. If you are single, you may feel a constant vigilance, fearing you may miss this elusive person. If you're in a relationship with someone, you may question if they are indeed "The One" or if you're settling for the wrong person. If a relationship ends with someone you believed to be "your person," you may fear you'll be alone forever or never experience love again.

The Hypervigilance Trap

Worrying about whether your partner is "The One" is a hypervigilance strategy the anxious part of your brain will use when you're in "survival mode." Remember, it's not the lack of certainty around your partner that's keeping you stuck—it's the belief you must have certainty around your partner.

Don't Fall Into This Trap

Think for a moment about ordering an entrée at a restaurant. (Obviously, choosing a partner and choosing an entrée are on a different caliber, but if you've been to a restaurant with an extensive menu—and you have anxiety—you'll understand this dilemma.) Picture yourself scanning the menu, torn between two equally appealing entrées. You make a split-second decision when it's your turn, and as the server walks away, the doubt already begins to creep in. When your dish arrives, no matter how delicious it smells and beautiful the presentation, rather than savoring each bite, you find yourself distracted—wondering if the other dish would've been a better choice.

Similarly, in relationships, the pursuit of the perfect partner can lead to second-guessing yourself. The person you're with may be incredible, satisfying the majority of your needs and desires. However, the belief in "The One" can make you question if there might be an even more perfect match out there.

Like the choice between two great entrées, society's promise of "The One" is a trap. Had you ordered the other entrée, you'd likely be feeling the exact same way. Similarly, if you choose a different partner, the doubt would still exist. Relationship anxiety manifests less because of who your partner is, and more because of how your brain analyzes who your partner is.

Certainty vs. Confidence

So how is it possible that so many people have found "The One" if it is indeed a relationship unicorn? While everyone's journey to love unfolds differently, and there are the occasional stories that do mirror a Hollywood love story, these are rare—and still imperfect! If you've ever heard someone saying, "I knew they were the one when…" and began feeling the pressure to have a similar certainty about your partner, it's important to recognize that even this person did not have absolute certainty in their relationship. Instead, what they had was *confidence* in their relationship—such confidence that they were able to proclaim they had found "The One." They chose to accept the inevitable degree of uncertainty that comes with any relationship and risked moving forward with confidence and self-trust anyway.

Someone Special

Rather than focusing your time and energy on whether or not you're with *the* one, consider figuring out if you're with *some*one special you could build a secure and enjoyable relationship with. Shift your expectations away from fairy-tale ideals and toward the qualities that will help you build a fulfilling life.

While no one can have complete certainty in their decision-making, we can all have confidence in our decision-making. And, yes, that includes you! Just as you can have confidence in your dinner selection and enjoy your meal without knowing for sure how the other entrée would've tasted, you can enjoy your relationship without knowing for sure if your partner is the *best* fit for you. It is possible to find someone special without eliminating every other person on planet Earth.

Use Cognitive Reframing to Shift Your Mindset

When you find yourself caught up in a line of questioning around whether or not you're with "The One," one of the ways you can get off the hamster wheel of doubt is to reframe the questions you're asking yourself. Much like a photo can look different depending on how it's framed, so too can thoughts. Cognitive reframing is a technique to shift your mindset and perspective on a situation, event, or emotion. While the situation, event, or emotion itself remains the same, adopting a different point of view can shift its meaning, interpretation, or significance. That new approach can help take anxiety out of the metaphorical driver's seat of your life. A few examples of cognitive reframing around questioning if your partner is "The One" include:

Current Question	Reframed Question
Is my partner "The One"?	Do my partner's values align with mine?
Does my partner dress stylishly enough?	Does my partner show care and kindness toward me?
Will my partner love me forever?	Does my partner share my vision for the future?
Do my friends think my partner is boring?	Do I enjoy spending time with my partner?
Is my partner really a "good person"?	Does my partner demonstrate accountability and a willingness to grow?

Rather than ruminating on questions that you will never find an answer to, asking yourself questions that have identifiable data points can help empower you to take the next best step.

Note: As you ask yourself these questions, consider them in the context of "most of the time"; for example: Does my partner show care and kindness toward me *most of the time*? Remember that no one is perfect and no relationship will be in perfect harmony all the time.

Exercise:
What Are Your Expectations of an Ideal Partner?

It's essential to understand your personal expectations of "The One." If your idea of the "perfect" partner doesn't account for the ups and downs of the human experience, you'll be setting yourself up for disappointment in partnership—even if you're with the person of your dreams. Follow these steps:

1. Take some time to write down which beliefs and expectations about "The One" you've adopted from the people in your life, the media, and/or society.
2. Review this list, considering whether these expectations have increased or decreased your level of joy, peace, and satisfaction in dating and relationships.
3. Ask yourself, "How can I reframe any expectations that contribute to decreased satisfaction to better accommodate the inevitable imperfections, disappointments, and periods of disconnection?"

For example:

- "My ideal partner and I will never disagree" sounds much more realistic when it's stated as "We will prioritize open-mindedness and respectful communication during disagreements."
- "My ideal partner will know what I need/want without me having to tell them" sounds much more realistic when it's stated as "They will take a genuine interest when I share my needs and wants and will be open to meeting them to the best of their ability."
- "My ideal partner and I will always feel in love" sounds much more realistic when it's stated as "We will focus on maintaining kindness, commitment, and acts of love in our relationship, even during challenging times."

MYTH NUMBER THREE:
SETTLING IS ALWAYS A BAD THING

Myth: Settling in a relationship is a negative thing and means you're receiving less than you deserve.

Fact: We all settle in relationships. Settling with intention can increase confidence, connection, and relationship satisfaction.

Unpopular opinion coming your way: There is nothing wrong with settling. We all settle, all the time. The truth is, we have to settle, because we can't have everything.

Imagine winning an all-expenses-paid getaway for one week to any destination in the world. You have ten dream destinations but only one trip. Is settling on one destination a negative thing? No. Can you still have an incredible trip even though there are nine places you're not visiting? Of course! If it's possible you would enjoy visiting another place just as much (if not more), should you stop yourself from enjoying the destination you chose? I hope not.

The stress of picking one destination could stop you from choosing any at all, but that would be settling too. It would be choosing to settle on not having *one* great experience just because you can't have *every* great experience.

While choosing a travel destination may seem less significant than choosing a partner, a similar concept applies: You can't have everything, but you can have everything you need to have an enjoyable, meaningful, and memorable experience. If essential elements are missing from a partner, then of course settling may not be in your best interest. This is where learning how to settle with intention can be helpful. You want to be willing to accept less than perfection—but not less than you deserve.

Settling for Less

When we think of settling, it's usually in terms of settling for "less than" something. In the context of relationship anxiety, think of settling as accepting less than certainty and perfection. Since pursuing perfection is exhausting and pursuing certainty impossible, settling is actually a wonderful option. It gives you permission to be satisfied with the choices you make regarding your relationship without knowing for sure they're the absolute "best" choices.

If you're feeling some anxiety at the mere consideration of embracing the idea of settling for less than perfection, remind yourself that this doesn't mean you're throwing all your standards out the window. Think of adopting a mindset that's searching for "great enough." You deserve, and are capable of creating, a "great enough" relationship! This type of partnership meets your must-haves and nonnegotiables, satisfies most of your value-aligned wants and needs, and has all the qualities necessary to create a stable and secure partnership. It may be below perfect but well above the mediocre "good enough."

Think of a "great enough" mentality as striving for A- or B+ work. To you perfectionists who are instantly filled with panic at the very thought of anything below A+ work, pause and take a long, slow, deep breath. Now ask yourself, "How has life constantly chasing perfection been going for me?" Since you're reading this book, it's unlikely to be working out well for you, at least when it comes to relationships. There is so much peace, joy, freedom, connection, and stability in giving yourself, and your partner, permission to be imperfect. While it can be difficult to let go of these ideals, in the long term, it's actually far more difficult to continue to hold on to them. One way to begin letting go of your perfectionist ideals is through learning how to settle with intention.

Settling with Intention

Settling with intention is a skill that can help you shift from feeling disempowered to empowered in your relationship. The key is learning to settle using your values—rather than your ever-changing thoughts and feelings—as a guide. Settling with intention also involves:

- Gaining clarity on what is *most* important to you in a relationship.
- Understanding what your must-haves and nonnegotiables are and not settling for less than those.
- Being open to accepting that your partner meets everything you absolutely *need* in a relationship but may not meet every single thing you'd *like* in a relationship.

Remember, settling is unavoidable, but it is the way you choose to settle that will lead to increased or decreased satisfaction in your relationship. Disempowered settling stems from a place of low self-worth, fear, and limiting beliefs. Empowered settling stems from a place of confidence, self-trust, and acceptance. Following are examples of empowered versus disempowered settling:

Disempowered Settling
- I have to lower my standards because the type of person I want would never be interested in me.
- I doubt I'll find someone else who loves me, so I should stay with this person.
- I'll compromise my nonnegotiables since this person/relationship has some great qualities that I would miss if we weren't together.
- I don't want to be embarrassed or let anyone down by breaking things off, so I should make it work.
- I'm getting too old/we've been together too long to start over.

Empowered Settling
- I'm willing to accept the parts of our relationships where we are not aligned because they are not deal-breakers for me.

- While my partner does not meet all my needs, I can have these needs fulfilled elsewhere (with friends, family, hobbies, etc.).
- My partner has some areas for improvement that I see them actively choosing to working on.
- I'm choosing to let my partner's shortcomings go because I feel more peace and less resentment when I do.
- I'm happy.to choose this person even though they're not perfect because overall I am content in my relationship.

> Case Study: Balancing Social Preferences

Jack and Rochelle bonded over shared interests in literature, cooking, and outdoor activities. As their relationship progressed, a noticeable difference in their social preferences emerged. Rochelle's extroverted nature clashed with Jack's homebody tendencies.

Understanding how important it was to Rochelle, Jack did his best to attend as many social gatherings as he could despite his preference to stay in. Rochelle appreciated Jack's willingness to accompany her to many events but couldn't help but feel disappointed when he declined an invitation. She also felt guilty, as though she was making Jack do something he didn't want to do. Despite having many shared interests and values, Rochelle's anxiety began to take over, and she wondered if she was settling by being with Jack.

During a vulnerable conversation, Rochelle realized that while she valued Jack's presence at social gatherings, she could also find fulfillment with friends and family even if he wasn't there. She recognized that her love and connection with Jack outweighed her desire for a more social partner. Choosing to prioritize mutual consideration and understanding, they crafted a balance between shared and independent activities.

Their decision to stay together exemplifies empowered settling. Rochelle acknowledged that while Jack didn't fulfill all her needs, the ones he didn't meet were not deal-breakers. She began to view each time he did accompany her as a generous act of love and recognized that the love and connection they shared surpassed their differences.

Settling with Confidence

Viewing settling as an empowered choice rather than a disempowered consequence can bring you increased clarity and shift your perspective on your relationship significantly. While it's deeply human to desire a perfect partner, if you can accept that you *are* settling, you'll no longer worry that you *might be* settling. Remember that it's less about if you're settling, and more about what you are, and are not, willing to settle for.

When you find yourself worried about settling, you can instead confidently say to yourself:

- I am settling for an imperfect partner I love and choose to be with each day.
- I'm choosing to be with a partner who meets the majority of my needs and desires in a relationship.
- I am settling with a partner who is caring, honest, communicative, funny—*and* who is often running late.
- While there may be another person I could also have a great relationship with, I am choosing to be content with my current partner because our relationship is very rewarding.
- I am settling for an imperfect partner who is pretty darn great.

Exercise:
Relationship Vision and Values

Before you can be confident in settling with a value-aligned partner who satisfies your must-haves and nonnegotiables, you need to know what those are. This exercise prompts you to explore key aspects of your relationship, providing you with a vision that aligns with your core values. The information you discover can help ground you when you're feeling anxious, support you in decision-making, and allow you to better articulate your relationship needs and expectations with your partner.

Core Values

Write down your top ten to fifteen core values. If you are unsure of your core values, you can use value lists, value cards, or value assessments to help you narrow them down. These tools can readily be found online, or, for a values exercise, see *Dare to Lead* by Brené Brown, PhD, MSW shown in the Resource List at the the end of this book for guidance.

Relationship Vision

Once you've identified your top ten to fifteen core values, begin writing your relationship vision. Consider how these values align with the following categories, noting any desires, preferences, boundaries, and deal-breakers. For example, if advancing in your career is a strong value of yours, your relationship vision may include having a partner who supports your career ambitions, is open to relocating with you if you're offered a promotion, and/or is on the same page regarding children or childcare. If faith is a strong value of yours, your relationship vision may include a partner who prioritizes faith, joins you in worship, and/or is on the same page regarding raising a family with a strong spiritual foundation.

- Career and Ambitions
- Communication
- Conflict Resolution
- Deal-Breakers and Nonnegotiables
- Emotional Support and Mental Health
- Education
- Faith and Spirituality
- Family Planning
- Financial Goals and Management
- Health and Wellness
- Home and Living Arrangements
- Intimacy and Sexuality
- Leisure and Free Time
- Personal Growth
- Social Life and Friendships
- Technology and Social Media
- Timelines and Milestones
- Travel and Adventure

MYTH NUMBER FOUR:
YOU CAN CONTROL YOUR RELATIONSHIP

Myth: If you are able to control your partner's behavior, you can avoid feelings of discomfort and feel more secure in the relationship over time.

Fact: Attempting to control your partner's behavior provides an illusion of control that worsens anxiety and creates disconnection over time.

During moments of anxiety, the urge to control can feel like a lifeline. Attempting to control not only your own thoughts and feelings, but also other people, may even become a coping mechanism. Even the most loving person can find themselves hounding, nitpicking, or resorting to manipulation in an attempt to ease their anxiety. This is especially true if you're experiencing relationship anxiety.

Anxiety promises you that if you just think, plan, anticipate, or catastrophize a little bit more, you'll find the answer or secure the outcome you desire. If you've ever felt this temptation, you are not alone. The belief that you can manipulate the outcome of your relationship is alluring! You may think, "If I just do this, say that, and change that, we'll be happy." Unfortunately, this provides only a false sense of security, not a truly secure partnership. A healthy, secure partnership *does* involve control—but probably not in the way you're thinking.

The Origin of Your Impulse to Control

When you find yourself being critical or focusing on your partner's flaws, it's often a reflection of your own discomfort rather than their behavior. That's because feeling out of control internally often leads to an impulse to control things outside yourself. While this strategy might work in some cases, it isn't the healthiest approach when the thing you're attempting to control is your partner. For example:

- If you're feeling anxious that people will judge your partner's style and it will reflect poorly on you, you might try to control what they wear.
- If you have an underlying fear that your partner might die young and you'll be alone, you might hound them about their diet and exercise routine.
- If you feel worried that your partner might drink too much alcohol at a party and do or say something embarrassing, you might tell them not to drink.
- If you fear that your partner will realize they don't miss you while on a friends' trip, you might tell them not to go on the trip.

If you've ever felt or acted similarly, go easy on yourself. Although these examples may appear to be about your partner's choices, they primarily reflect your own feelings.

What You *Can* Control

Once you understand that your internal discomfort is leading your urge to control, it makes sense that the "controlling" to do here is not external—it is to go inward. You'll need to acknowledge your feelings and fears and change *your* behavior. In your relationship, you're only in control of yourself: your actions, responses, and decisions. Your partner's thoughts, actions, feelings, and decisions are beyond your control. Ironically, acknowledging this doesn't diminish the control you have over the outcome of your relationship but enhances it!

While initially difficult to accept, you'll likely notice a sense of freedom and autonomy in accepting that despite your best efforts, you only have so much control. Let's take the example of your partner's outfit. Your choosing an outfit for them takes away their autonomy. It robs them of an opportunity to express themselves. It may leave them feeling like you don't trust their judgment or aren't attracted to them. The consequence of this may be that you notice them sullen or pulling away a bit—which only makes you feel more anxious.

Consider how this attempt to control also reinforces to your brain that other people's judgments and opinions of your partner are significant. Does what others think of your partner's clothing mean more to you than what your partner thinks of their own clothing? This fixation on external opinions can lead to feelings of insecurity and undermine the trust and autonomy within your relationship.

Additionally, while you may believe that controlling your partner's behavior will alleviate your discomfort, it often leads to unintended consequences. Your attempts to control may backfire, resulting in increased anxiety, feelings of disconnection, and a loss of control over the relationship dynamics in the long run. A healthier and more sustainable alternative to controlling your partner is to let your partner be themselves and to feel your feelings that come along with it.

Feeling Your Feelings As an Alternative to Control

Let's explore a different scenario. Imagine if instead you let your partner pick their outfit. Maybe it's not your favorite style, but instead of telling them to change, you say nothing at all and accept the fact that while you love this person, you are *not* loving their outfit. You allow yourself to feel the emotions of anxiety, disgust, judgment, or embarrassment that may arise when seeing their outfit. As you practice tolerating the emotions that arise, rather than controlling your partner, you may begin to see the situation differently.

As an alternative to requesting an outfit change, depending on how comfortable each of you is with poking fun, you could respond playfully by joking about their outfit. Or you might approach the situation with genuine curiosity, asking what they love most about their outfit. In making one of those choices, you practice creating space for your feelings and surrendering the need to control while also learning more about your partner and supporting their self-expression. It's a win-win!

Consider the last time you felt the urge to control a situation in your relationship. What were the underlying emotions driving this impulse? Was there an opportunity to let yourself feel these emotions without attempting to control your partner? If so, how might the outcome have been different?

Communication over Control

Allowing yourself and your partner to be fully authentic and accept individual responsibility for decisions, mistakes, and consequences fosters peace, mutual growth, and confidence. By releasing the need to control every detail, you open space for spontaneity and unpredictability where you and your partner can problem solve as a team. This approach helps build a more connected and resilient relationship.

Ultimately, "staying in your lane" is an act of love. Of course, you can still make requests of your partner and offer them suggestions. While vulnerable communication is an integral part of a healthy, secure partnership, there is a difference between making a request of your partner with loving-kindness and trying to control their decisions.

It's through relinquishing control that you learn more about one another, understand how to navigate life together, and how to decide if the relationship is aligned with your values or not. Inviting your partner to grow and change—while being willing to do the same yourself—leads to more favorable results than attempting to force change on them.

MYTH NUMBER FIVE: LOVE IS A FEELING

Myth: Love is a feeling that will always be present if your partner is right for you.

Fact: While the *feeling* of love may come and go to some degree, in healthy relationships love is much more than a feeling. It is a multifaceted embodiment of respect, commitment, dedication, effort, play, laughter, forgiveness, flexibility, hope, boundaries, and vulnerability—qualities that are important to nurture both within yourself and in your relationship with your partner.

Think of one of your favorite movies—one that's a source of joy and familiarity. Maybe it's a film you've watched over and over. Now, imagine a day when, for no particular reason, you're not in the mood to watch it. Maybe you try to watch it and the punchlines don't seem as funny, or your attention drifts elsewhere and you want to turn it off. Does this mean you no longer love the movie? Does this mean you *never* really loved the movie? Does this mean you will never enjoy watching the movie again? Not at all. It could simply mean this is a favorite movie of yours that you're not in the mood to watch today.

Just as your favorite movie may not resonate every single day, feelings of love toward your favorite person too can experience ebbs and flows.

Is Love a Feeling?

While you certainly can feel love, it's crucial to understand that love surpasses mere emotion—it is an action, a decision, and a commitment. Being in love with your partner is knowing you love them and behaving like you love them, even on the days when the feelings aren't as prominent.

No one is in a constant state of feeling love. In fact, no one experiences any single emotion all the time. Feelings are inherently dynamic. Just as feelings of happiness and anger come and go, so do feelings of being "in love." This doesn't mean you're falling in and out of love with your partner. Similarly to how you can be confident you love a particular movie and not be feeling it one day, so too can you be confident you love your partner but not be feeling it at the moment.

While you can't control your feelings, you are in control of your actions. This means you can make the choice to act in loving ways toward your partner even in the moments you are not experiencing overwhelming *feelings* of love. Feelings aside, love is something you must repeatedly choose to commit to and build on—or let go of—as you continue to get to know one another and experience life together.

Feelings Are Not Facts

When it comes to feelings, keep in mind that while they provide valuable information, relying on them as the sole decision-makers in relationships can lead to confusion and doubt. The transient nature of feelings is one of the reasons that relationships built on feelings alone rarely have depth or longevity. As important as they are, emotions function to reflect your interpretation of a situation rather than the objective truth. With this in mind, while your feelings are always valid, they're not always based in fact. Making relationship decisions based on your values—rather than your feelings—will bring you far more assurance in your partner and your relationship.

Give Yourself Permission to Feel Indifferent

There is a profound freedom that comes with giving yourself permission to feel indifferent, blah, or even turned off by your partner at times. If you can accept this is an expected part of healthy, secure relationships, you can free up an incredible amount of time and energy that would otherwise be spent analyzing your feelings and your partnership. It can also free up mental bandwidth to reflect on more productive questions, such as "Are you loving *yourself* at the moment?"

During moments when you feel off or disconnected, it's common to spring into "fix it" mode. Your brain is looking to find something to pin your feelings on, and if you have relationship anxiety, your relationship becomes the easy target. Sometimes your relationship *is* the culprit, but many times it's not. Going inward to gain clarity rather than immediately fearing there is something wrong with your relationship can help provide a reset. Next time you're experiencing an absence of love toward your partner, consider asking yourself some reflective questions, such as:

- Have I been nurturing my own well-being lately?
- Have I been engaging in personal hobbies or activities that bring me joy and fulfillment?
- Am I content in other areas of my life right now outside my relationship?
- Am I unfairly expecting my partner to "make" me feel better?
- Am I experiencing extra stress through work, family, finances, illness, etc.?
- Am I actually experiencing healthy stability in my relationship, but it feels unfamiliar because I'm used to chaos and toxicity?

Your relationship with yourself sets the tone for your connection with, and feelings toward, your partner, so if you notice several of these areas could use some personal TLC, you may want to start there.

The Difference Between Love and Infatuation

Let's be real—we all want to love and be loved! However, that coveted "in love" feeling often stems more from the chemical and hormonal surge of infatuation than from genuine, enduring love. Understanding the difference between infatuation and lasting love is key in navigating the inevitable fluctuations of emotions. While infatuation tends to peak quickly and weaken with time, it's important to note that waning infatuation doesn't diminish the depth and strength of the love that can develop over time, especially in secure and committed relationships. This also does not mean you won't ever have feelings of infatuation again as the relationship progresses—but it does mean you won't *constantly* feel that way in your relationship. And that's a good thing!

It's perfectly natural to feel different toward your partner a year in than you did during your first month of dating. While it's completely expected to experience varied feelings about your partner over time, mundane human moments can stir doubt in those with relationship anxiety. Perhaps you've noticed this come to the surface in your own life with questions like: "Why don't I get butterflies anymore?" "Why don't we talk as long on the phone anymore?" "Why don't we want to have sex as often?"

The truth is, while instant chemistry and feelings of infatuation can be fun to experience, they are not strong predictors of the health and longevity of a relationship. Love, contrary to what the fairy-tale portrayal would like you to believe, is not something that is instantaneously found and everlastingly kept. It is something that you and your partner consciously build and finesse over time.

Is Love Really All That You Need?

Love is undoubtedly important, yet it alone cannot sustain a thriving partnership. A healthy relationship requires more than romantic feelings. Your love should complement the foundation built on each of your values and nonnegotiables. If you've *never* experienced love or attraction toward your partner—and these elements are important to you—sure, it might indicate that the relationship is not aligned with your needs. On the other hand, if you're navigating a period of diminished love or attraction, focusing on some nervous system regulation work (see Chapter 1) and revisiting your relationship vision and values might be a more aligned action to take.

Remember, constant feelings of love are not a prerequisite for a strong and lasting connection. It's the alignment of values, the commitment to growth, and the willingness to weather the ebbs and flows of feelings together that form the foundation of a truly fulfilling relationship.

Key Takeaways

- True love is built over time, not found in one magical moment. Idealized narratives of love perpetuated by the media and society are often unrealistic and can lead to feelings of inadequacy in real relationships.
- Aim to settle for someone who shares your core values and relationship vision and who you can build a meaningful connection with rather than focusing solely on romantic feelings.
- Feelings of love will vary in intensity over the course of your relationship, and love alone does not make or break the relationship.

CHAPTER 3

EXPLORING THE BEHAVIORS KEEPING YOU STUCK

The tendency to overthink, dissect, and give unnecessary meaning to the nuances of relationships is all too common: "They probably aren't even interested in me. Did I say something wrong? Are they mad at me?" We've all been there, caught in the web of self-doubt, wondering if our actions or inactions have jeopardized a connection. However, if you find yourself stuck in this web often, you'll continue to struggle to feel secure in your partnerships. This chapter will help you understand some of the most common behaviors responsible for keeping you stuck—such as doubting everything, constantly seeking reassurance, and even avoiding certain situations—and learn what you can do instead to begin to break free.

WHY IT'S IMPORTANT TO BREAK THE CYCLE OF ANXIOUS BEHAVIORS

It's a frustrating paradox: trying to think your way out of overthinking. And yet, that's exactly what so many people with relationship anxiety find themselves doing. For those navigating their relationship alongside anxiety, overthinking becomes a futile effort to understand, predict, and control the future of the relationship. However, this attempt is like dousing fire with gasoline and expecting it to go out. You can't worry your way out of worrying or analyze your way out of overanalyzing any more than you can dampen a roaring fire with gasoline.

As you read the first two chapters of this book, you might have found yourself resonating with the words, yet still feeling uncertain about your relationship. This is, in part, because overcoming relationship anxiety is not just about understanding where the anxiety originates; it's also about understanding—and shifting—the patterns and behaviors that perpetuate the cycle. Your attempts to secure certainty (via overthinking and other behaviors) may instead actually be reinforcing your feelings of doubt and uncertainty. Ironically, the more deeply you believe you must know if you partner is right for you before you can be content in the relationship, the less content you'll ever be. This chapter will help you identify and reframe behaviors and get yourself out of this never-ending loop.

HOW TO DEAL WITH INTRUSIVE THOUGHTS

Before we delve into which specific behaviors are keeping you stuck, let's discuss in general why you might have developed these behaviors in the first place—starting with intrusive thoughts. Intrusive thoughts are thoughts that are unwanted, distressing, and/or ego-dystonic, which means the thought is in opposition to your beliefs, morals, and values. (For example, you might have the thought "What if I cheat on my partner?" while you deeply value fidelity and integrity.) The discomfort from such thoughts can cause you to take action in the form of behaviors that, unfortunately, only reinforce anxiety.

How Intrusive Thoughts Often Appear in Relationships

Everyone gets intrusive thoughts, not just people with relationship anxiety. However, not everyone gets stuck on these thoughts. Many people can have an unwanted thought and think to themselves, "Hmm, that was an unwanted/unusual/unpleasant thought," and then let it go and move on with their day. For someone with anxiety and/or OCD, letting the thought go and moving on feels difficult—if not impossible.

If you're someone who gets stuck on intrusive thoughts, these thoughts or feelings can be scary and make you anxious. Naturally, you want to get rid of them! You might feel like you need to know where the thought came from, what it means about you or your partner, and if what the thought is telling you is really true or not.

For example, imagine you're on a date with your partner. You're having a great time and feeling connected, until a group passes by and you involuntarily have the fleeting thought that someone in the group is attractive. Having the thought that someone else is attractive while you're on a lovely date with your partner could be unwanted and distressing. This thought then triggers the fight-or-flight response, raising your anxiety level and leading to a cascade of questioning, such as:

- Why would I think someone else is attractive?
- Does that mean I don't think my partner is attractive?
- Does that mean deep down I don't love them?
- Did I just cheat on my partner?
- Am I a terrible person who is leading them on?
- What if my partner thinks other people are more attractive than me?
- Is this a sign we shouldn't be together?

All the while, your anxiety is increasing, your confidence in your relationship is decreasing, and the present moment of enjoying a sweet, connected date with your partner gets completely hijacked by your doubt and anxiety.

Intrusive Thoughts Lead to Compulsive Behaviors

In moments like this, many people are tempted to give in to a compulsive behavior (sometimes called a safety behavior), which is an action you feel driven to do in an attempt to make yourself feel better when you're feeling anxious or uncertain. Such behaviors are often done repetitively if you're in a state of distress. You might be so accustomed to engaging in these behaviors when feeling anxious that they become automatic. Examples of these behaviors include reassurance seeking, avoidance, checking, and rumination. In our example, compulsive behavior might look like:

- Leaving the event so you don't again see the person you thought was attractive.
- Confessing to your partner you just found someone else attractive.
- Imagining cheating on your partner to check how you "feel" about it.
- Asking your partner if they've ever found someone else attractive.

One of the many downsides to these compulsive behaviors is that they bring only temporary relief. You might feel better in the moment, but the next time you feel uncomfortable—which could be a day later or a mere hour later—your brain has learned that it should engage in these behaviors again to feel better. It knows no other way to move forward. Not only is living this way exhausting, but it also doesn't ultimately bring you the long-term comfort or certainty you're seeking.

You may be wondering, "Are these behaviors really *that* bad? What's wrong with wanting to feel better!?" There is, of course, nothing wrong with wanting to feel better. However, engaging in compulsive behavior when you're in an anxious spiral falsely reinforces to your brain that you cannot handle feeling anxious, uncomfortable, or uncertain. It teaches your brain that it has to control and dissect your thoughts, because they are all significant. And that is incorrect. Why? Because...

Intrusive Thoughts Are Essentially Meaningless

The truth is, thoughts are meaningless until you assign them a meaning. Finding another person attractive has no bearing on whether or not you find your current partner attractive, nor can that thought or feeling alone tell you if you're meant to be with them. That means it is not the thought itself that causes the distress; it is the meaning and significance you assign to the thought and the actions you take in response that can lead to feelings of doubt and sometimes even panic.

Believe it or not, you *do* know how to let go of thoughts already. By some estimates, people have roughly fifty thousand thoughts per day. That's a lot of thoughts you don't have time to play detective around, and you seamlessly let most of them go every day. See? You're already adept at letting insignificant thoughts go. *You* get to decide which ones are worthy of your conscious attention and which ones are not. When you're on a date with your partner and you're distracted by intrusive thoughts, you're taking time and energy away from being present to all your other thoughts, including the potentially loving and connecting thoughts toward your partner.

Now let's take a closer look at some of the more common compulsive behaviors that are keeping you stuck, along with behavior modification techniques that can help bring lasting confidence rather than temporary relief when you're feeling anxious.

REASSURANCE SEEKING

We all have moments when we question ourselves and our relationships. In these moments, seeking reassurance can promote trust, comfort, and security. That could sound like asking a question once, accepting the answer, and moving forward. However, when reassurance seeking morphs from a desire for genuine support into a desperate need for frequent certainty and relief, it can be more harmful than helpful in overcoming anxiety.

Compulsive reassurance seeking isn't a straightforward process. It becomes a looping pattern, where each attempt to gain answers only invites more questions. Any immediate relief the reassurance offers is quickly overshadowed by new doubt. This behavior creates a cycle that actually makes your anxiety worse. For example: You ask your partner if they're upset with you because you notice they've been quiet. They respond that they're just tired. In a secure exchange, this response would suffice, and you'd move on. However, in a reassurance-seeking loop, you might persist, asking repeatedly if they are sure or if they would tell you if they were upset.

After they assure you several times they are not upset, rather than experiencing relief, your anxiety could morph, setting off a cascade of new doubt. You might start to think, "I often ask them if they're upset with me. Maybe they weren't upset, but now that I asked if they were, they're probably annoyed with me now for asking." This spike in doubt and anxiety prompts further attempts to seek reassurance, leading to statements like "I'm sorry I'm so annoying" or "I just want you to know you can tell me if you're upset with me."

Seeking answers directly from your partner is just one of the many manifestations of compulsive reassurance seeking. Some other examples of how seeking answers for reassurance could show up include:

- Endless Internet research around how to know if your partner loves you, what is "normal" in relationships, and how to know if you're with "The One."
- Reading books and articles on relationship anxiety to see if the doubt you're experiencing is due to anxiety or a genuine mismatch in compatibility.
- Posting in or searching Internet forums to see if other people are experiencing the same thoughts/doubts you are.
- Asking your partner hypothetical questions out of "curiosity, not worry" (for example: "If I were in a coma, would you stay

OVERCOMING RELATIONSHIP ANXIETY

with me?", "Would you jump in front of a bullet for me?", or "If we met ten years earlier, do you think you would love me?").

- Consulting family, friends, therapists, coaches, religious leaders, or psychics and mediums for feedback on your relationship.
- Asking others about their relationships to ensure that what you're experiencing is "normal."
- Venting or confessing thoughts and assessing your partner's response and/or body language.

Don't Overdo Healing Either

If you notice you're using *this* book in search of reassurance or answers regarding the "rightness" of your relationship, consider taking a break. Even consuming "self-help" information compulsively can hinder your progress. Put the book down, take a breather, and return when you're feeling more centered and able to approach and apply the tools effectively.

Tip for Change: Try Seeking Support Rather Than Reassurance

Asking for support is different than essentially demanding reassurance, and it's more likely to lead to you feeling better in the long term. For example, say you're feeling anxious about your partner's commitment to the relationship. Reassurance seeking might sound like repeatedly asking questions such as: "Do you *really* love me? Are you sure you want to be with me?" Support seeking, on the other hand, could sound like saying, "I've been feeling insecure lately and could really use a hug," or "I've been having a tough time with some anxious thoughts and could use some encouragement." Support seeking involves understanding, collaboration, and shared solutions through vulnerable communication, while reassurance seeking tends to focus on seeking immediate relief through eliminating doubt.

CONFESSING

Confessing your thoughts, worries, dreams, or fantasies is another behavior commonly associated with relationship anxiety. Like reassurance seeking, confessing is sometimes done in an attempt to make sure your partner is not upset with you. However, it can also have a moral component to it, where you're feeling guilty, shameful, or "dirty," and you feel the need to confess as a way to "cleanse" yourself and atone for your thoughts. Such feelings of guilt or shame can stem from something known as Thought-Action Fusion.

Thought-Action Fusion describes a way that your brain attaches undue importance to your thoughts, and it can affect you in two different ways:

1. It can make you believe that having a thought increases the likelihood of that thing happening. As an example, imagine that as your partner is leaving for work, you have an intrusive thought of them getting in a car accident. You might believe they're now going to get in an accident and it is your fault because you had that thought.

2. It can lead you to believe that thoughts and actions have the same moral consequences. For example, you might have a dream where you cheat on your partner and feel as guilty as if you had actually cheated on them in your real, waking life. You might feel as though you have been unfaithful, and you worry this could mean you are a bad person and/or do not love your partner.

Both of these scenarios would understandably bring up feelings of anxiety and discomfort. In an attempt to minimize that discomfort and absolve your guilt, you might feel the urge to confess your thoughts or dreams, hoping to receive forgiveness and wipe out any negative consequences from these "dangerous" or "immoral" thoughts.

Tip for Change: Practice the Pause

Each time you have the urge to confess, try sitting with the discomfort of not confessing for as long as you can. You can even start with a few seconds if that's all you can do! Keep trying to work your way toward not confessing at all. Each time you delay a compulsive behavior, it gives you the opportunity to strengthen the "muscle" of tolerating, rather than eliminating, discomfort.

AVOIDANCE

Avoidance is exactly what it sounds like: the act of staying away from situations, environments, people, or topics that make you uncomfortable, in an attempt to not feel anxious. While avoidance is a natural—sometimes lifesaving—behavior, when used as a compulsive coping strategy for anxiety it's only going to reinforce your anxiety in the long term.

Avoidance can show up as:

- Turning down invites to events where there will be "happy couples."
- Not watching movies with passionate sex scenes or actors you find attractive.
- Avoiding certain topics of conversation that are triggering, or changing the subject if your partner brings them up.
- Choosing not to share significant needs or feelings with your partner.
- Having a hard time committing to (or ending things with) your partner.
- Avoiding being physically or emotionally intimate with your partner.
- Avoiding dating all together.

Keep in mind that sometimes avoidance is a good thing. If you genuinely are not interested in something, saying "no" can be an act of self-care and self-respect. For example, if you do not want to be sexually active with your partner due to personal, value-aligned reasons, choosing to say "no" to having sex is not avoidance; it is healthy boundary setting.

However, if you genuinely do want to have sex with your partner but are feeling anxious that you might have intrusive thoughts while being intimate, or you're worried about how you might look, smell, or taste, turning down opportunities for intimacy is probably compulsive avoidance. Avoidance is an unhealthy coping strategy when something seems interesting, fun, and/or value aligned, but you avoid it due to worries that it may trigger doubt or anxiety. In such cases, you end up prioritizing your anxiety over your personal values and desires.

Tip for Change: Gradually Expose Yourself to Difficult Things

Instead of avoiding certain situations entirely, try to break them down into smaller steps you feel better able to handle. For instance, if dating triggers anxiety, and your ultimate goal is marriage, start with more manageable steps like joining a dating app, creating a profile, or initiating a conversation. As you gain confidence at each step, progress to more challenging tasks, such as meeting someone in person or committing to a long-term relationship. This gradual exposure technique not only helps you confront situations you might have otherwise avoided, but it also allows you to build self-confidence. This approach to confronting your fears is inspired by techniques used in Exposure and Response Prevention (ERP) therapy, which is an evidence-based treatment for OCD and anxiety disorders. You can refer to the Resource List at the back of this book for more information on ERP.

CHECKING

Checking, or testing yourself or your partner to see how you feel, is another compulsive behavior that may be keeping you at the mercy of relationship anxiety. Checking is similar to reassurance seeking in that they both involve searching for information to bring a sense of relief. However, while reassurance seeking typically involves consulting someone else for answers, the checking compulsion involves consulting yourself. This behavior generally entails directing your attention inward to a thought, feeling, or sensation in an attempt to provide self-reassurance. Checking in this sense can show up as:

- Checking to see if you feel "in love" with your partner.
- Checking to see how you feel toward other people and how that compares to how you feel toward your partner.
- Assessing your partner in situations with friends and family to make sure they're pleasant, fun, and intelligent enough.
- Observing how other "happy couples" interact to see how you and your partner's interactions compare.
- Imagining scenarios where you get married, break up, go on vacation, or have children to test how you would "feel" about it.
- Cuddling, kissing, having sex, or being intimate in some way to check for feelings of arousal or emotional connection.
- Breaking up with your partner to see if you feel sadness or relief.

The idea behind these behaviors is that you're checking for thoughts and feelings that indicate love and connection or the lack thereof. However, this leads you to analyze and intellectualize your feelings rather than *feel* them. The more you're checking to see how you feel, the less present you will be to how you're actually feeling.

Tip for Change: Name How You're Feeling

When the urge to check your (or your partner's) feelings hits, instead name how you're feeling in the moment. (If you're having trouble deciding, look online for a feelings wheel or list of feelings.) You may notice you're feeling worried, insecure, uncertain, inferior, etc. When you recognize the feeling behind the urge to check, you can practice sitting with that feeling instead of checking on your relationship. This simple practice shifts your focus inward, helping you understand and process your emotions and ultimately empowering you to move forward. Remember that feelings aren't facts and all feelings are temporary!

RUMINATION/MENTAL REVIEW

Rumination is when you focus on a particular thought, feeling, experience, or memory for periods of time beyond what is helpful. Reliving past conversations in your mind or overanalyzing your or your partner's actions is a very common behavior that can keep you stuck in relationship anxiety. While we all grapple with rumination from time to time, it's important to recognize that this thinking pattern can be emotionally draining and distressing—and is ultimately unhelpful.

Rumination differs from healthy self-reflection in that reflection is constructive processing done with the intent of learning and growing. It leaves you feeling empowered to make positive change. Rumination gives the illusion of being productive, without actually being helpful. Thinking about something again and again makes your brain think it's getting closer to certainty when you're really going in mental circles.

Some ways rumination could be showing up in your life include:

- Reviewing your first few dates to see if you missed any red flags.
- Replaying conversations in your head to ensure you came across authentic.
- Reflecting on awkward things you said and being hard on yourself about it.
- Thinking back to things you did/said after a relationship ends, wondering if the relationship would have turned out differently if you had done/said things differently.
- Thinking back to see how you felt about previous partners to compare to how you feel about your current partner.
- Replaying dates and intimate moments to ensure you weren't awkward.

- Replaying situations to make sure you didn't accidentally flirt with someone while you were out and about.
- Replaying the brief encounter you had with the barista, wondering if you missed your opportunity at finding "The One."

The key to keep in mind with rumination is that no matter how many times you replay scenarios, what's done is done. Whether you come to the conclusion that you handled the situation beautifully or that you massively messed it up...there's nothing you can do about it either way. Your time and energy are far better spent moving forward than ruminating on where you've been. While this is certainly easier said than done, you do have control over whether you choose to keep ruminating or not!

> Case Study: Ruminating in Action

Abby and Rachel had been dating for a couple of weeks. They had only had a handful of dates so far, but Rachel could see potential. The two had tentative plans to meet up after work, and Abby told Rachel she'd call her at 5 p.m. to confirm details. As 5:04 p.m. approached and there was still no call, Rachel could feel her heart racing and palms sweating. By 5:06 p.m., she was sick to her stomach and called Abby hoping for some relief, but there was no answer.

Rachel immediately began reviewing their recent interactions in her mind: "I knew I shouldn't have shared that story with her the other day; it was stupid. I shouldn't have responded so quickly to her text either; I must've come across desperate. Or maybe I waited too long, and she thinks I'm not interested. Maybe she was going to call, but now that I called her, she is annoyed and doesn't want to call. Did I ruin this? Why am I so awkward?! I mess everything up."

Rachel's self-deprecating commentary was interrupted when, at 5:08 p.m., Abby called, saying, "I'm so sorry. I'm running behind; I got caught up with a client and my phone was at my desk. It's nice to hear your voice. Are we still on for tonight?" Rachel's racing thoughts began to subside, replaced by a sense of relief and excitement as she and Abby confirmed their plans for the evening. She recognized that ruminating on the things she did or did not say only led to unnecessary stress without providing any real benefit.

Tip for Change: Incorporate More Balanced What-Ifs

As you're mentally reviewing past scenarios, your brain is probably getting stuck on thoughts such as "What if I sounded stupid?" or "What if I had deeper feelings for my ex?" To offset these sticking points, give your brain an additional perspective to challenge the automatic negative assumption. For example, transform a thought like "What if I sounded stupid to them?" to "What if I sounded interesting to them?" Or swap "What if I had deeper feelings for my ex?" for "What if I'm about to experience the deepest feelings I've ever felt for someone?" This mental shift can help you entertain both negative and positive possibilities, break the cycle of rumination, and promote a more constructive thought process over time.

Exercise:
Thought and Behavior Log

Now that you have an idea of some common behaviors that might be keeping you stuck, take a moment to reflect on your own life. When you're feeling anxious, what do you tend to do? Whether you have noticed some of the behaviors discussed showing up in your life, or you have not have paid much attention to your behavior patterns up to this point, this exercise can help bring a deeper awareness to them. Grab a notebook or open a new note in your phone and:

1. Keep a running list for twenty-four hours of all the doubtful, obsessive, or intrusive thoughts that pop up. (Note: If your doubt and anxiety show up less frequently, consider keeping a running list for one week as opposed to twenty-four hours.)
2. If you notice yourself responding with a behavior to make your feelings of anxiety go away (reassurance seeking, avoidance, checking, etc.), write that down as well.

Increasing awareness around your current behaviors is a crucial first step so you know where you stand now. We will expand on this exercise in an upcoming chapter in Part 2 of this book.

SACRIFICING LONG-TERM GAIN FOR SHORT-TERM COMFORT

If you notice yourself engaging with some of the behaviors you've learned about in this chapter, go easy on yourself. There is a reason you've adopted these responses as your go-tos when you're feeling anxious: They work...temporarily. The problem is that while they may bring short-term comfort, they lead to long-term anxiety. Your brain has been doing the absolute best it can to help you feel safe and secure using the skills it has available. However, as you're hopefully learning, not only do these compulsive behaviors strengthen—as opposed to reduce—anxiety, but they also can take a toll on your relationship.

Choose (Short-Term) Discomfort

While overcoming relationship anxiety, choosing temporary discomfort can lead to long-term gain! Be willing to tolerate discomfort that may cause your anxiety to spike temporarily but ultimately teaches your brain not to fear discomfort. This strategy helps you gain more peace and fulfillment long term.

FOCUSING ON WHAT YOU *WANT* IN A RELATIONSHIP

A common point of fear and frustration for those experiencing anxiety around their relationship is worrying that their anxiety itself is going to push their partner away. If you've ever felt this way, first know that your anxiety is not your fault, and it does not mean you're unlovable or undeserving of a flourishing relationship. It is absolutely possible to have a healthy, connected relationship alongside feelings of doubt and anxiety, and you deserve a partner who is supportive and accepting!

That said, even the most patient, loving, and understanding partner may struggle with repeatedly hearing your doubts around your love for them or theirs for you. This isn't because you are annoying or a burden but because your partner is human as well, with their own complex needs, emotions, and desire to feel secure in partnership.

With this in mind, incorporating the Tips for Change discussed in this chapter rather than engaging in compulsive behavior can bring more peace and confidence to you—and your partner. While there remains an inevitable degree of uncertainty in every relationship, you have the power to decide whether you're going to fixate on the possibility of your relationship not working out or invest in the possibility of it working out. Don't be more committed to what you *don't* want than to what you *do* want.

Key Takeaways

- Overcoming relationship anxiety involves embracing discomfort and uncertainty instead of resorting to compulsive behaviors for temporary relief. By acknowledging and accepting discomfort as a natural part of growth, you can break free from the cycle of doubt and cultivate genuine confidence in your relationship.
- Anxious, intrusive thoughts are meaningless until you assign them a meaning. While you can't control the presence of your thoughts, you can control which thoughts you assign importance to, which thoughts you engage with, and which thoughts you deem insignificant.
- Relationship anxiety has the potential to affect not only the person experiencing it but also their partner. Repeated attempts to ensure connection can actually lead to disconnection.
- Note that while self-help strategies like those discussed in this book can provide significant support, if Part 1 has illuminated areas where you feel you could use more individualized support, see the Resource List at the end of this book for additional guidance and/or consider working with a professional who has training and experience in working with relationship anxiety.

NAVIGATING RELATIONSHIP ANXIETY

Welcome to Part 2 of *Overcoming Relationship Anxiety*, which will explore a range of topics aimed at helping you look forward and navigate specific challenges that may accompany relationship anxiety. From redefining what constitutes a healthy relationship to cultivating trust, presence, and effective communication with your partner, Part 2 focuses on fostering resilience, curiosity, communication, and vulnerability. The chapters ahead will also highlight the importance of living in the present moment, building trust within yourself, and swapping judgment for curiosity. Plus, we will touch on how grief, loss, and forgiveness are essential parts of any healing journey, both in relationships and in life. These principles will all strengthen the foundation of healing laid out in Part 1.

By the end of Part 2, you'll gain clarity on the importance of making value-based decisions and understand that while you cannot predict every twist and turn ahead, you can be confident in your ability to handle them, regardless of which direction they take. You'll leave this part feeling soothed, nurtured, confident, and capable of making decisions for your life, trusting that you will love, learn, and be okay, no matter what.

As in Part 1, each chapter in Part 2 features exercises that will personalize the guidance for your own unique relationship journey, as well as case studies of sample situations that might resonate with you. By engaging with the content and utilizing the tools and insights provided, you'll be better equipped to embrace the presence of anxiety without allowing it to dictate your actions. You will have the knowledge and strategies to enjoy your relationship more and worry about it less!

CHAPTER 4

WHAT IS A "HEALTHY RELATIONSHIP"?

Life can sometimes feel like a decision-making marathon. Think about your daily routine: From the moment you wake up to the time you go to bed, how many decisions do you make? From smaller decisions like what to eat or when to head to bed, to more significant ones like whether or not to accept a job offer or book a vacation, it may feel like you're constantly assessing and deciding. Studies estimate that adults make tens of thousands of decisions daily—no wonder decision-making can be downright overwhelming, especially if your nervous system already feels worn down.

What do decisions have to do with a healthy relationship? Well, imagine tackling these thousands of decisions hand in hand with your partner—*and* expecting to be in agreement with each one. That'd be impossible, right? But if you're someone who prefers constant alignment—as many people with relationship anxiety do—the inevitable disagreements may leave you feeling uneasy and questioning if your relationship is on the right track. If this is you, you may take comfort in knowing that being in constant harmony and remaining perfectly in sync are not the true measure of a healthy relationship.

This chapter will explore the essence of what *does* make for a healthy relationship: tenets like respect, boundaries, and solid communication. It will also guide you through the nuances of conflict, shed light on some positive aspects of disconnection, and help you distinguish between normal rough patches and toxic behavior. If you're someone who finds conflict unnerving, this chapter will offer new perspectives and tools to feel more confident through the inevitable moments of both connection *and* disconnection.

DEFINING A "HEALTHY RELATIONSHIP"

Defining a healthy relationship is a really personal thing. Yet, within individual preferences, certain key elements are at the heart of almost all healthy and secure relationships. For example, partners mutually express kindness, admiration, and respect, and are met with acceptance and understanding when sharing needs, feelings, desires, and boundaries. This space allows both partners to be authentic without fear of retribution.

That said, remember those myths discussed in Chapter 2—relationships aren't fairy tales, and your partner isn't flawless. They are an imperfect human being, prone to making mistakes, just like you. That's why healthy relationships also include space for disagreements and conflicts to be resolved. Let's take a deeper look at some of the hallmarks of respectful and strong partnerships, such as boundaries, conflict management, communication, and forgiveness.

BOUNDARIES

Setting a boundary is the process of clearly defining what is and isn't acceptable in the relationship. Boundaries allow you to maintain autonomy and self-expression, and they empower both partners to honor their needs, assert preferences, and protect limits within the relationship. Setting, enforcing, and respecting boundaries are fundamental to fostering mutual respect and emotional well-being in relationships.

You can set boundaries in various aspects of the relationship, including physical, emotional, sexual, psychological, financial, and spiritual realms. They serve as a means to ensure you feel safe and valued within the partnership.

While at first it may feel uncomfortable or even "mean" to start implementing boundaries, that couldn't be farther from the truth. Recognizing and communicating boundaries is not an act of selfishness but rather an act of care for both partners. When you and your partner honor each other's boundaries, it shows consideration and appreciation for each other's individuality, preferences, and well-being. In turn, that environment nurtures feelings of trust, acceptance, and understanding and therefore helps minimize anxiety-inducing situations. It also provides you and your partner with the opportunity to grow together, as setting clear boundaries helps reduce misunderstandings and conflict.

How to Set a Boundary

Setting a boundary is as simple as communicating your request in a clear and respectful way. Another essential aspect of boundary setting is clarity on the consequences of not respecting a boundary combined with enforcement of those consequences. For instance, a complete boundary may sound like "I love watching our show together at night, and I need to be in bed by 11 p.m. in order to get up semi-rested for work in the morning. If we don't start the show by 9:30 p.m., you're welcome to watch it without me, but I won't be able to join you that night."

It's crucial to follow through with the consequences to maintain clarity and integrity in boundary setting—meaning, if your partner isn't ready to watch until 10:15 p.m., don't join them. Without following through, your partner may learn that you don't mean what you say, and this can lead to frustration, confusion, and misunderstanding downstream. That's why the follow-through is the most important part of boundary setting!

Boundaries Are Not the Same As Control

Especially in the context of relationship anxiety, it's essential to recognize that setting boundaries isn't about controlling a partner or avoiding vulnerability. Instead, it's about advocating for your emotional well-being and fostering a relationship that's built on trust, respect, and authenticity. For example, there is a difference between saying, "If we don't start the movie by 9:30 p.m., I'm not going to watch it" (boundary) and "If we don't start the movie by 9:30 p.m., you can't watch it" (control). Of course, you can make requests of your partner, but you cannot set a boundary to control their behavior, only your own.

When both partners' boundaries and the consequences for breaking them are clearly communicated, it encourages mutual understanding. It also provides valuable information if boundaries are crossed, allowing for necessary adjustments and growth in the relationship.

Don't Automatically Label Behavior You Don't Like As Toxic

In recent years, there's been a trend toward labeling everyday human behaviors as toxic or problematic. This societal shift can amplify feelings of uncertainty around the "rightness" of your relationship. Take setting healthy boundaries, for example, which is sometimes unfairly labeled as controlling. Or instances where different recollections of events are misinterpreted as gaslighting. Or the desire for attention misconstrued as narcissistic behavior. These behaviors alone don't necessarily signify red flags. Context matters, and perfection is an unrealistic standard for any relationship.

MUTUAL RESPECT

Knowing how to identify relationships that feature mutual respect is an important skill to have as you move forward. Amid the influx of self-help advice, the suggestion to cut out "toxic people" from your life has likely crossed your path. While sound advice for many, if you're wrestling with relationship anxiety, the pressure to cut out "toxic people" might trigger a spiral of doubt. Red flags aren't always obvious, and distinguishing potential red flags from normal imperfections is crucial.

Keep in mind that even in the healthiest relationships, partners may goof up; they may crack a joke that stings or show a hint of control or jealousy. These behaviors might be labeled as red flags or toxic in specific circumstances but could also be nothing more than a healthy partner having an imperfect human moment. You may again find yourself looking for certainty here, wondering how to discern a red flag from a flawed human moment. While no definitive criteria exist, there are some key distinctions.

Toxic vs. Healthy

In the face of disagreements and disconnection, a *toxic* partner is more likely to:

- Blame or deny.
- Gaslight and/or insist you "need help."
- Raise their voice or stonewall.
- Make empty promises with no action or changed behavior.
- Exhibit these unhealthy behaviors repeatedly.

A *healthy* partner who made a mistake is more likely to:

- Take accountability.
- Atone for their inappropriate action.
- Express a desire to do better.
- Seek support to heal if necessary.
- Follow up their words and apologies with action and changed behavior.

Individuals grappling with relationship anxiety may unintentionally minimize their partner's unhealthy behavior, putting the blame on themselves instead. (For example, thinking, "If I was more understanding, they wouldn't have gotten so angry.") This stresses the importance of distinguishing between healthy relationship dynamics and toxic patterns when addressing relationship anxiety.

If doubt and anxiety persist despite being in a reliably healthy and secure relationship, it requires a different response than if it persists in a toxic relationship. If your partner's behavior is generally healthy, consider embracing some minor discomfort rather than immediately seeking to change your partner. Conversely, if doubt surrounds a relationship where you regularly see toxic or abusive behavior, experiencing anxiety would be a healthy response to mistreatment, not something to overcome. Here, contemplating the "rightness" of the relationship would be an appropriate response.

While figuring out what behavior is normal imperfection and what is toxic may initially trigger *more* feelings of uncertainty, the information you're gathering in this book will gradually bring clarity to the distinction between the two and instill self-confidence that you know which is which.

EMBRACING CONFLICT AS A TEAM

Imagine planning a two-day road trip without accounting for pit stops—no gas, no food, no rest breaks. If this is your approach, you won't complete your journey and/or you'll be disappointed when someone has to go to the bathroom. That's also what it looks like when you attempt to have a relationship without assuming conflict will happen. Encountering conflict is as normal and necessary in healthy relationships as pit stops are on a road trip—the key is that healthy relationships are able to manage this conflict in a safe and respectful way.

Rather than viewing conflict as an inconvenience diverting you from your destination, it can be reframed as a necessary stop on the road to keep you thriving on that road long term. Just as you're going to get only so far in your trip if you refuse to stop for gas, you can experience only so much depth and connection if you're unwilling to embrace conflict in your relationship. Acknowledging that conflicts will happen—rather than being shocked or scared when it arises—is like stopping for fuel on a road trip.

Look For More Positive Than Negative Interactions

When it comes to relational health, shifting your focus from *if* you disagree to *how*—and *how often*—you disagree can be more clarifying and productive. Through his research with couples, psychologist John Gottman, PhD, developed a method where he was able to predict with 90 percent accuracy whether couples would divorce or stay together. As part of this research, he found that stable, healthy relationships have a 5:1 ratio of positivity to negativity during conflict. This means that for every negative interaction, healthy relationships have five or more positive interactions.

Negative interactions include:

- Being emotionally dismissive, critical, or defensive.
- Disinterested body language, such as eye-rolling or turning away.
- Being distracted, such as scrolling through the phone as the other speaks.
- Walking away, hanging up, or otherwise ending a conversation prematurely.
- Resisting what Gottman calls bids for connection (for example, refusing a hug or kiss).
- Stonewalling or withholding attention or affection for hours/days after a conflict.

Positive interactions include:

- Making eye contact, nodding in agreement, turning toward their partner, and/or saying, "Uh-huh" where appropriate to indicate interest and attention.
- Being curious.
- Offering an apology when necessary.

- Thanking their partner for sharing.
- Validating their partner's feelings.
- Bringing levity to the situation where appropriate.

Gottman believes that it is not the presence of conflict, but rather the absence of positive, connected interactions to balance out the negative interactions, that leads to the demise of relationships. When handled in a mature and healthy way, conflict can actually leave you feeling *more* connected to your partner. Disagreeing with maturity requires accountability, vulnerability, care, and curiosity. Those are all elements that can help you feel prouder of, and more confident in, yourself *and* your partner.

Give Yourself Permission to Argue

Whether you're dealing with anxiety, have a history of trauma, or witnessed poor examples of handling conflict when you were growing up, it's understandable if you're someone who would prefer to avoid conflict altogether. But since a partnership involves two complex and dynamic individuals, expecting to sync up with your partner all day, every day, is impossible. This isn't to say that you will be encountering conflict at every turn but that moments of disagreement and disconnection are an inevitable and integral part of healthy relationships.

In fact, the absence of disagreements is actually not indicative of a healthy relationship. It generally means that one or both partners are not sharing their needs, preferences, or full authentic self with the other. This is in part why couples who "never fight" tend to have *less* fulfillment and longevity than those who get on each other's nerves from time to time. Withholding your true feelings, trying not to make waves within the relationship, and/or dismissing hurt without addressing it leads to feelings of resentment and loneliness. Giving yourself permission to risk conflict with your partner can actually help you feel more connected.

Giving yourself permission to argue with your partner doesn't mean it's okay to be physically or emotionally cruel or abusive toward one another. It is granting yourself moments to be annoyed, frustrated, and at odds with one another. When your body feels safe to encounter conflict, it can continue to see your partner as your teammate, remain grounded, and focus on solutions and growth. When your body feels triggered by conflict, it sees your partner as the opponent, feels threatened, and focuses on fight-or-flight.

Take a Team Approach to Conflict

When conflict arises within the partnership, it's important to remember that it is you and your partner against the problem at hand, not you and your partner against one another. You remain a united team, and as teammates, you work together toward resolution. This allows you to focus less on who is right and who is wrong and more on how to reconnect with this person you love and care about.

Another important thing to keep in mind is that not all conflicts have tangible solutions your team is going to agree on. Sometimes, the "solution" is having a respectful dialogue where you hear one another out and agree to disagree and move forward. Conflict without a solution doesn't mean your relationship is doomed. The real "win" in an argument is getting back to a place of harmony with your partner, not proving them wrong. When focused on reconnection, rather than being "right" during disagreements, it's more likely you will engage in more positive than negative interactions, bringing you closer to that 5:1 ratio. This in turn increases the likelihood of relationship success and the amount of time you spend in harmony.

The Power of Gratitude

Expressing gratitude toward your partner is a great way to boost the number of positive interactions you have together. Take time each day to acknowledge and appreciate their efforts, big or small. Research shows that practicing gratitude promotes positivity and strengthens emotional bonds, creating a deeper sense of connection, even during moments of conflict.

Don't Avoid Conflict to Protect Your Partner's Feelings

It's natural to want to protect your partner's feelings and shield them from any potential hurt or disappointment. You may even be afraid to express your own feelings if they might hurt your partner. However, discomfort and vulnerability are inherent aspects of healthy relationships. Sometimes it's appropriate for feelings to be hurt—not in a malicious or intentional manner but as a byproduct of honest communication and growth. Sharing something significant with your partner that inadvertently causes discomfort presents an opportunity for deeper understanding and connection. It allows both of you to learn more about each other's needs, desires, and boundaries, which can foster empathy and feelings of safety.

Connect, Then Correct

Before addressing grievances with your partner, prioritize connection. Begin by remembering that you're on the same team and express appreciation or empathy (where appropriate) to establish a receptive atmosphere. Connecting before you attempt to correct reduces defensiveness, encourages a smoother conversation, and increases the likelihood the conversation will go well.

Experiencing discomfort or guilt can also be a catalyst for personal growth and introspection—yours and/or your partner's. It prompts you to reflect on your actions, principles, and communication patterns, encouraging you to strive for greater alignment with your morals and values. For example, if your partner lets you down or otherwise hurts your feelings, you may be tempted not to tell them because you don't want them to feel bad for hurting your feelings. However, their temporarily feeling bad would be an appropriate response to learning that they hurt the feelings of someone they care about. It provides an opportunity for repair and gives them a chance to learn so they don't repeat this behavior in the future.

Instead of avoiding difficult conversations or tiptoeing around sensitive topics, embrace them as opportunities for growth and deeper

OVERCOMING RELATIONSHIP ANXIETY

connection. Remember, it's okay to feel bad momentarily—it's a natural part of the learning process. By allowing yourself and your partner to experience discomfort in a supportive and compassionate environment, you encourage authentic communication, personal development, and a stronger bond. Plus, this situation provides an opportunity to gain clarity on whether or not you're truly in a healthy partnership. Your partner's response to your sharing your authentic feelings provides an opportunity to assess whether they exhibit more behaviors of a healthy or a toxic partner.

Practice Direct Communication

One way to have healthy conflict (or avoid it in the first place) is to be mindful of how you're communicating with your partner. Not all communication is created equal. Relationship anxiety often leads to overthinking and overanalyzing, which can result in subtle hints to or from your partner being misinterpreted. While it may feel safer to drop hints rather than directly expressing your needs, this approach often leads to frustration and resentment when your partner doesn't pick up on them.

Direct, assertive communication is essential for building healthy communication habits in relationships. Direct communication involves openly expressing your thoughts, feelings, and needs in a straightforward manner. It also prioritizes honesty and acceptance, allowing both partners to speak without fear of judgment or ridicule. Let's now explore five key elements for healthier communication: mindful timing, using "I" statements, active listening, validation, and agreeing where you can. These strategies can help you cultivate healthier, more fulfilling relationships in the face of relationship anxiety—plus, you can gather valuable information about your partner's behaviors and communication style. This can help you gain more clarity on which areas of the relationship the two of you align and which areas have room for improvement.

Consider Your Timing

Before initiating a conversation, consider whether it's the right time for both you and your partner. Avoid starting deep discussions when your partner is busy or distracted, as this can lead to miscommunication and frustration. Ensure that both of you have the physical time and mental energy to dedicate to the conversation.

Use "I" Statements

Utilize "I" statements to express your feelings and needs—that way, you are stating facts without blaming or accusing your partner. Instead of saying, "It's obvious you don't love me anymore because you never kiss me goodnight," try sharing, "I feel loved when you kiss me goodnight. Is there a reason you haven't been doing it this last week?" Your partner is less likely to get defensive, and you're more likely to make connections together. This approach allows you to take ownership of your feelings, encourages open dialogue, and fosters understanding between partners.

Practice Active Listening

Practice active listening by fully engaging with and understanding your partner's perspective. Give your full attention, maintain eye contact, and show empathy and interest in what your partner is saying, both verbally and nonverbally. Remember, listening to understand, rather than to respond, is crucial for effective communication. Instead of automatically formulating your response or rebuttal as your partner is talking, simply focus as objectively as possible on what they're saying.

Validate Their Feelings

Validate your partner's feelings by acknowledging and accepting them, even if you don't necessarily agree. For example, if your partner shares with you that they're feeling unloved, rather than saying, "Don't be silly, of course I love you," you could say, "That sounds really painful.

I do love you very much, but I hear that it's not coming across in the way you need right now." Demonstrate empathy, understanding, and support, which can strengthen emotional connection and trust within the relationship. Avoid dismissing or minimizing your partner's feelings, as this can lead to resentment and distance.

Agree Where You Can

In your everyday communication, focus on areas of agreement rather than disagreement. Acknowledge where you align with your partner's perspective, even if you don't agree on everything. Instead of immediately defending yourself against accusations, start by acknowledging any valid points your partner makes. This approach promotes a sense of teamwork and collaboration, emphasizing you're both on the same side, working together to solve problems. For example, imagine your partner expresses that you obviously don't care about them or their time because you've been late for the last five dates. Instead of responding with "That's not true; I was only late *three* times," start by acknowledging what you can agree on, perhaps: "You're right, I have been late more than I would like over the last few weeks, and I'm sorry about that."

> Case Study: Conflict and Compromise

Carl and Derek, who have been dating for two years, found themselves in a heated argument over how to manage their finances. Carl, a meticulous planner, wanted to create a strict budget to save for their future. Derek, more spontaneous and carefree, preferred to enjoy their money in the present. Their conflicting approaches to finances led to tension and frustration, with both feeling misunderstood and unappreciated. Carl felt that Derek was irresponsible and didn't take their financial future seriously, while Derek felt that Carl was too controlling and didn't value his input.

As the argument escalated, they realized that they were stuck in a cycle of blame and defensiveness and were unable to see each other's perspective. They agreed to take a time-out and revisit the conversation when they were both calmer and more receptive to each other's viewpoints. During this time, they reflected on their own values and priorities, acknowledging they had different perspectives shaped by their upbringing and experiences.

When they reconvened, Carl and Derek instead approached the conversation with empathy and openness, actively listening to each other's concerns without judgment. They found common ground by realizing that they both wanted the same thing: financial security and happiness, although through different means.

Through honest communication, they were able to find areas where they could compromise. Derek agreed to put aside some money each month for retirement, recognizing the importance of long-term financial planning. Carl agreed to allocate a portion of their budget for biweekly dinners out, understanding Derek's desire for spontaneity and enjoyment in the present. They left the conversation feeling proud of themselves for working together as a team and felt even more connected than they did prior to the disagreement. Carl and Derek's approach used empathy, respect, and curiosity to turn a conflict into an opportunity for growth, understanding, and deeper connection.

FORGIVENESS

Forgiveness is a powerful part of healthy relationships and often naturally follows the practice of healthy communication and emotional expression. It presents both partners with an opportunity to release resentment, heal wounds, and reconnect after a difficult time.

A common pitfall in relationships is the tendency to keep score, clinging to past transgressions as a measure of accountability. While the motto "Forgive but don't forget" may be helpful for some, when you have relationship anxiety, it's essential to recognize the cathartic power of letting go. Releasing the mental (or physical) tally of past mistakes frees up emotional space for genuine forgiveness and new experiences untainted by the past.

Forgiveness is not an acknowledgment that past actions were acceptable; rather, it's a conscious choice to liberate oneself from the burden of resentment and bitterness. It's about reclaiming control over how you respond to your thoughts and feelings rather than letting your partner's actions or inactions dictate them for you. Through embracing forgiveness, you have an opportunity to shift away from the cycle of blame and anger and move toward growth and healing.

A critical component of forgiveness is compassion—for both yourself and your partner. It requires acknowledging human fallibility and accepting the imperfection that exists within your relationship. By extending compassion and grace, you open the door for greater trust, intimacy, and emotional resilience.

Practicing forgiveness is sometimes easier said than done. As you work toward cultivating this practice within your relationship, it's important that you express forgiveness only when you truly mean it. If you tell your partner you forgive them and are ready to move on, it's crucial that you do not bring up the offense with them again in the future. This can lead to frustration and distrust within the relationship. It's okay if it takes you some time to be ready to forgive, but do your best not to communicate forgiveness if you're not yet there.

While forgiveness does not erase the scars of the past, it releases them from dictating and clouding your future. Releasing the weight of past hurts offers a pathway to peace and reconciliation so you can enjoy your relationship in the future.

Exercise:
Conflict in Review

Honestly reflecting on past conflicts can give you valuable insight into how you might handle things differently next time. This exercise encourages you to reflect on a recent disagreement or conflict you experienced with your partner to identify areas of improvement. Follow these steps:

1. **Revisit the conflict:** Take a few moments to recall a recent disagreement as accurately as it happened. Write down the details of the situation, including what triggered the conflict, how both you and your partner responded, and what the outcome was.
2. **Reflect on the communication dynamics:** Consider how effectively you and your partner communicated during the conflict. Did you both engage in active listening and express yourselves openly, or did defensiveness take over? Did you aim to understand each other's perspective or try to correct each other? Did you prioritize reconnection or prioritize being right? Consider if the two of you focused on proving your points or on genuinely listening to each other's viewpoint.
3. **Identify areas for improvement:** If the conflict didn't resolve smoothly, rewrite the scenario as you wish it had gone. Envision how you could have approached the disagreement differently to promote understanding and connection. Focus on practicing reflective communication, acknowledging your partner's perspective, remembering you and your partner are teammates, and seeking common ground where possible.
4. **Revisit with your partner:** At a time that's good for both of you, share your reflections with your partner. Do your best to focus

OVERCOMING RELATIONSHIP ANXIETY

on things you learned about yourself. Share areas where you've identified ways you could have acted/responded differently rather than immediately pointing out where your partner could have improved.

Key Takeaways

- Conflict is an inevitable part of any healthy relationship; it's how you handle it that matters most. Embracing conflict as a team with maturity and empathy can lead to deeper understanding and connection with your partner.
- Establishing and respecting boundaries is fundamental to fostering mutual respect and emotional well-being in healthy relationships. It's not about control but rather about creating a safe space for both partners to be authentic and express their needs.
- Direct and assertive communication is essential for building healthy relationships. Utilize "I" statements, practice active listening, and prioritize empathy and validation to encourage open dialogue and mutual understanding.

CHAPTER 5

BEING PRESENT

Imagine you're watching a movie. One minute after it starts playing, you ask yourself, "Do I like this movie? Am I enjoying it so far? Did I make a good selection?" As the movie continues, you begin to analyze every sentence and facial expression: "Was that a good line? Could it have been delivered differently? Why would they make that face?" You then start to fixate on the actors and wonder if they were really the best casting choice for the part. You search on your phone to learn what other movies they've acted in, and before you know it, you're reading about their entire life story. And then the movie ends. You wonder, "How is the movie already over!?"

How much of the movie did you see, and how much did you miss due to your thinking, checking, and analyzing? Would you even be able to make a fair assessment of how you feel about the movie at the end? For many people with relationship doubt and anxiety, this is similar to how their time with their partner is spent. The constant cycle of thinking, judging, observing, and testing doesn't leave a lot of time for experiencing the present moment. This chapter will explain what it means to be present in your relationship, help you get to the bottom of why you may be struggling with being present, and offer practical strategies you can begin using today to stay in the present moment more consistently.

THE ART OF BEING PRESENT

When you're watching a movie, you don't check in with yourself every two minutes to see if you're enjoying it. You can assess how you felt about it when it's over. You can also trust that if you're totally *not* into the movie, you'll know that without having to pause every few minutes and consciously check on your feelings. This exemplifies the art of being present. When you're truly present, your feelings come more naturally and authentically. When you're forcing or searching for feelings, it's far more difficult to know how you authentically feel. The same is true in relationships.

Are You Behind the Glass?

If you find yourself struggling to be present, it might feel like you're observing your own presence in the relationship through a thick plate of glass. It's an odd form of self-observation where you're watching yourself engaging in desirable activities, yet you're so entangled in judgments, questions, and critiques that fully experiencing the present moment becomes a challenge.

This can be an incredibly frustrating and disorienting experience. Even if you desperately want to be more present and to feel authentic and connected, you might find that the more you check to see if you're being present, the less present you feel. This is because thinking about being present and truly *being* present are two different things.

As you work toward being more present in your relationship, that "glass" will gradually become thinner, until you're fully immersed in the present moment without feeling like you're observing from behind glass at all. Then you'll no longer be observing yourself in the moment but fully living it. You'll no longer be contemplating responses, just responding authentically, in the moment. Your experiences will likely feel fuller and more intense. Removing that protective layer of "glass" may leave you with more uncomfortable feelings at times, but there will be many more comfortable feelings too. You will learn that experiencing your relationship in real time is far superior to critiquing your relationship every step of the way.

> Case Study: Lost in Analysis

As the holidays approached, Cameron found herself so excited at the thought of sharing her first holiday season with Isaiah. She scouted the best holiday photo spots and activities in anticipation and envisioned days filled with laughter, twinkling lights, and the magic of the season. She longed to experience the holiday love other couples enjoyed.

However, when they headed out to take pictures by a decorated tree, the reality was different. The cold and the crowds seemed to overshadow the festive spirit. Instead of basking in the magic, Cameron found herself questioning: "Are we in love right now? Am I having fun? Is this how others feel?" Cameron's mind was elsewhere.

As they headed home, rather than feeling connected and chatting about their day, Cameron found herself editing their tree photo to share with others. Instead of bursting with love, she found herself scrutinizing Isaiah's body language in the photo and questioning whether or not they were even happy when the photo was taken.

In the end, a day that Cameron had eagerly awaited slipped away, lost to analysis and not being in the moment. She could hardly remember the lights and conversation, and the love and connection she had anticipated were overshadowed by constant questioning and critique. Cameron's experience reflects the balance between the anticipation of a special outing and the necessity of being authentically present to truly experience it.

What Does Being Present Look Like in a Relationship?

Being present isn't just about physically showing up; there is a difference between being in the same space with your partner and truly showing up for each other. When you are present in your relationship, you:

- Feel free from the judgment or commentary of your internal dialogue.

- Release expectation and comparison.
- Are focused on and engaged in the here and now. You don't assess whether or not you like the here and now; you simply allow whatever is present to fully and nonjudgmentally be.

As you begin to practice being more present, be patient with yourself. Remember, the expectation isn't to be present every waking moment—nobody achieves that. What matters is your effort and intention. With time, the more frequently you're present in your relationship, the greater the confidence and clarity you'll feel.

PRACTICE MINDFULNESS

Mindfulness is more than a buzzword; it is a practice that guides you away from constant analysis and rumination and anchors you in the current moment. Adopting mindfulness as part of your day-to-day interactions encourages you to engage with the present moment without judgment or expectation.

Mindfulness is similar to being present. Being present involves actively participating in the current moment, activity, or conversation, focusing on what is happening here and now without distraction. Mindfulness takes being present a step further by incorporating nonjudgmental awareness and acceptance of your internal experiences. In addition, being present is more about external engagement, while mindfulness is about being aware of and accepting your inner state while actively participating in the current moment. Mindfulness is not about analyzing or judging how you think or feel but rather noticing it and choosing to engage with the present moment, regardless of your thoughts or feelings.

Mindfulness is about accepting what is rather than what you wish things were. It is experiencing each moment fully, whether or not it's turning out the way you had envisioned. It's giving yourself the opportunity to view the whole puzzle rather than dissecting it piece by piece.

OVERCOMING RELATIONSHIP ANXIETY

Following are some strategies that can help you be more consistently mindful, and in turn present, in your relationship.

Embrace Neutrality

Adopting a mindset in which all your thoughts, feelings, and emotions are equal and acceptable allows your brain to take a break from passing judgment. Part of the judgment and preoccupation with checking your feelings moment to moment comes from having all-or-nothing thinking, for example: "If I feel happy, that's good; if I feel sad, that's bad." Try to gently remind yourself that there are no good or bad thoughts or feelings—they're all neutral.

Furthermore, remember that you can't control your thoughts and emotions, only how you respond to them. Since your responses can influence your thoughts and emotions, being mindful of your responses can help you move past anxious feelings. For example, acts of love and playfulness can boost love and connection, while acting distant and critical is more likely to lead to feelings of disappointment and disconnection.

Instead of assigning meaning to every thought and feeling, do your best to allow them to ebb and flow freely. You don't have to like all your thoughts and feelings, but you can choose to allow them to be there, without assigning them meaning. This neutrality is a key part of mindfulness.

Feelings alone are not a solid or reliable source when assessing the health and compatibility of your relationships, so feeling love doesn't mean your partner is right for you any more than feeling unsure means they're wrong for you. By creating equal space for all thoughts and emotions to exist, you'll feel more freedom to experience all the parts of your relationship.

Minimize Compulsive Behavior

Compulsive behaviors are the actions we take to alleviate discomfort or seek certainty, often diverting our attention from the present moment. Much of the time you're struggling to be present in your relationship is due to engagement with a safety or compulsive behavior, such as rumination, checking, thought suppression, or avoidance (see Chapter 3).

The harder you work at reducing compulsive behavior, the more adept you will become at tolerating uncomfortable thoughts and feelings. The better you get at tolerating these feelings, the less alarming they will be when they inevitably show up. The less you need to feel comfortable and certain in your relationship, the more open to the present moment you will become.

Practice Active Listening

Active listening is a great way to be mindful and stay connected to the present moment. When your anxious brain takes over, you might be listening to judge, listening to respond, or not listening at all. Active listening is about listening to learn, understand, and connect with your partner.

Here are some components of active listening to try out:

- Make eye contact.
- Nod in agreement where appropriate.
- Paraphrase back what you're hearing.
- Ask questions to learn more.

When you engage in the practice of active listening, you must be present to the conversation. Placing your focus on hearing your partner, rather than judging them (or yourself), is a great way to be mindful, and in turn present.

Reflect on Your Feelings after the Fact

Instead of assessing your emotions during an event, think about them later, when you decide is a good time. Set aside, say, thirty minutes

OVERCOMING RELATIONSHIP ANXIETY

to reflect on and assess your feelings. This practice will help your brain learn that there will be time for reflection and analysis but that *you* get to decide when that time is rather than your anxiety choosing for you.

Let's say you're taking a weekend getaway—rather than analyzing how you feel each moment of each day, set aside time to reflect when you get home from your trip. Think about the high points and low points of the weekend and decide if overall you had a fun time or not. This practice will not only give you more time during the weekend to be present to one another but also help you make a bigger-picture assessment rather than multiple microscopic assessments throughout the day.

If going a handful of days without thinking about your feelings seems too difficult to start, give yourself permission to take it day by day or hour by hour. Any amount of time you're able to remain present will help build new pathways and connections in your brain.

Start Ignoring Some Thoughts

You teach your brain what is important through which thoughts you choose to engage with. While trying to completely stop your thoughts from existing (thought suppression) is not an effective tactic, choosing not to engage with them will help lessen them over time.

Imagine your anxious thoughts and feelings are like a spam caller. Imagine you were in the middle of interviewing for a dream job and got a spam call. You might notice the call coming in, and could even be temporarily distracted by it, but you would quickly refocus on the conversation at hand because it's important to you.

Aim to safeguard your time with your partner in a similar way. You can acknowledge the thoughts and feelings vying for your attention but choose to metaphorically send them to voicemail rather than picking them up. Just as you wouldn't let a spam caller interrupt your interview, don't let spam thoughts interrupt time with your partner.

Focus on Physical Sensations, Not Feelings

If you're prone to spending too much time assessing your feelings, try shifting your focus to noticing sensations instead. Here are some ideas:

- When hugging your partner, notice the warmth and pressure as opposed to searching for feelings of love or attraction.
- When walking hand in hand, notice where your bodies are making contact with one another rather than comparing yourself to other couples walking by.
- If there is a moment of silence between you, notice the texture of the surface you're sitting on or the ambient sounds around you rather than analyzing the silence for meaning or significance.

This practice can shift your focus from the intellectual evaluation of the moment to a more mindful, sensory engagement with your partner.

COMMON TRIGGERS THAT PREVENT YOU FROM BEING PRESENT

Even if you want to be more present, you might find it difficult to achieve despite your motivation. This could be due to one or more triggers disrupting your ability to be present with your partner. Some of the more common triggers include:

- **Comparison:** Whether it's comparing milestones, social media portrayals, or perceived levels of happiness, constant comparison can trigger feelings of inadequacy and doubt, pulling you toward analyzing your relationship rather than living it moment to moment.

OVERCOMING RELATIONSHIP ANXIETY

- **Uncertainty about the future:** The fear of the unknown is a significant trigger for anxiety. Concerns about where the relationship is heading, uncertainties about commitment, or fear of potential conflicts can overshadow the present moment, making it difficult to fully engage with your partner.

- **Past trauma and experiences:** Previous relationship experiences—particularly negative or traumatic ones—may resurface, leaving you dwelling on the past rather than being focused on the present.

- **Fear of rejection or abandonment:** A fear of rejection or abandonment can create a perpetual cycle of seeking reassurance or fearing that one wrong move could lead to rejection. This loop can hinder genuine connection and presence.

- **Challenges with communication:** Difficulty in expressing needs, concerns, or emotions can create tension. Fear of miscommunication, conflict, or not being heard could prevent you from fully engaging in meaningful conversations and experiences with your partner.

- **Perfectionism:** The pressure for you or your partner to meet unrealistic expectations—whether self-imposed or influenced by external factors—can lead to constant evaluation and dissatisfaction, making it difficult to relax and enjoy the present moment.

- **Difficulty with letting go:** If you have a hard time letting go of the past, you might struggle to wholeheartedly embrace the present. Harboring resentment, hurt, or anger toward your partner makes it difficult to let your guard down to view their actions and behaviors objectively in the present.

- **Trust issues:** Doubting your partner's intentions, loyalty, or reliability can lead to hypervigilance and constant monitoring, preventing relaxation and intimacy.

- **Fear of vulnerability:** The fear of being hurt or rejected when expressing authentic feelings or needs can lead to being guarded and emotionally detached, hindering genuine connection and presence.

Do you notice yourself triggered by any of these factors in your own relationships? Recognizing your personal triggers empowers you to develop strategies to manage your anxiety. It also can safeguard against giving in to old patterns when faced with a trigger, ultimately leading to greater presence and connection in your relationship.

Are You Present Anywhere?

In your quest toward being more present in your relationships, it's worth taking a moment to first assess if you're truly present *anywhere* in your life. Perhaps your struggles to be present aren't solely about your partner. Being fully present demands time, energy, and an ability to prioritize. Consider whether your current level of stress and obligations might be impeding your ability to be fully present anywhere.

TAKE CARE OF YOURSELF

Do you find yourself burned-out? If you feel depleted, exhausted, and pulled in too many directions at once, you might need to rest and recharge. Being present in your relationship while mentally running through a never-ending to-do list is difficult. Before you dive into new techniques, it's critical to replenish your resources. After all, how can you expect to show up fully when your tank is empty? Taking care of yourself is a crucial aspect of being present in your relationship. It provides an opportunity to "fill your tank" so you have more energy to give to other areas of your life, including your relationship.

Even Fun Events Can Feel Draining

In addition to life's many demands, living with relationship anxiety can be draining in and of itself. Take, for example, hanging out with friends. Of course, that should be fun, but when anxiety takes over, the entire experience can be spoiled. Perhaps you've experienced something like this: You're out with your friends, but instead of fully enjoying their company, you find yourself comparing your relationship to theirs. Maybe you're wondering if your partner measures up to theirs or if your connection is as strong. In those moments, you're not really present. Your mind is elsewhere, caught up in a spiral of doubt and comparison. And it's likely not just happening among friends; even during solo activities like a morning walk, you might find yourself testing how you feel without your partner by your side rather than fully soaking in the alone time in nature.

When you're dealing with relationship anxiety, it's easy to lose sight of your own needs and well-being. Endlessly scrutinizing your relationship can leave you feeling inadequate, drained, and disconnected—all of which only means you need to nurture yourself even more. After all, being present with your partner starts with being present with yourself.

Rest and Recharge in Ways That Work for You

Making a point to engage in regular self-care as you work through your anxiety is essential. Self-care isn't just about bubble baths and face masks; it's rediscovering who you are beyond your relationship and carving out time for your hobbies, passions, and solo adventures. Look for moments where you can reconnect with your own thoughts and feelings in a nourishing way.

Whether it's losing yourself in a book, soaking up the tranquility of nature, or cuddling on the couch with your dog, moments of self-care are essential for recharging your emotional battery. Spending quality time with friends, free from the shadow of relationship comparisons, can also help you refill your tank. Remember, self-care isn't one-size-fits-all—focus on the hobbies and activities that leave you feeling more energized and happy, even if they're not the ones social media touts.

PRESS PAUSE ON HEALING

Sometimes, in the relentless pursuit of growth and healing, we forget to simply live and celebrate what we have and how far we've already come. It's all too easy to fall into the trap of tiresomely working on yourself or your relationship and get consumed by the idea you must always be actively "fixing" something. This mindset suggests there is an end point to healing, but the reality is, there is no end point. An important aspect of being present is giving yourself permission to take a break from the relentless need to figure everything out and just be where you are.

The healing journey is a continuous process, and that's okay. The point of growth and healing isn't just to fix your relationship; it's to fully embrace and enjoy your life and relationship as they are, starting today! You don't have to wait until you're fully healed to experience joy, love, and fulfillment. Allow yourself the freedom to let go of the pressure to always be working on your relationship or yourself. Instead, focus on being present in the here and now. After all, it's in the here and now where you'll find connection and happiness.

Exercise:
Celebrate the Ordinary

Bestselling author Mark Manson once said, "Extraordinary results are a matter of repeating ordinary actions over a long period of time. Start with ordinary." Embracing this philosophy can be so beneficial for managing relationship anxiety. Many of us overlook the value of everyday, "ordinary" gestures, assuming they are merely the bare minimum. In a world where we often expect more from our relationships, acknowledging the significance of these seemingly mundane actions might feel like a step backward. However, while grand gestures of love are certainly appreciated, it's the ordinary interactions that form the foundation of your life together.

For this exercise, make it a point each day this week to intentionally express gratitude for the "ordinary." While you don't *need* to thank your partner for simply pulling their weight, conveying appreciation can create a sense of connection and warmth for you both.

For instance:

- Does your partner take out the trash regularly? A simple acknowledgment like "It's so nice that I don't have to worry about taking out the trash. Thanks for taking care of that" can go a long way.
- Did your partner grab you a snack while they were at the store as they usually do? Expressing gratitude by saying, "I really appreciate it when you get me a snack. It makes me feel special to know you're thinking of me while you're out and about" can strengthen your bond.
- If your partner is typically running behind schedule and manages to be on time, rather than dismissing it or expressing surprise, try saying, "Thanks for being ready on time today. I see you making an effort to work on that, and I appreciate it."

Not only does showing appreciation strengthen your connection, but it also increases the likelihood those behaviors you welcome will reoccur. Being on the lookout for ordinary behaviors can help you become more focused on the present moment and appreciative of what you already have.

Key Takeaways

- Being present is a practice that involves doing your best to fully and nonjudgmentally engage with your partner, allowing experiences to unfold naturally, without the need to analyze or evaluate each one. As soon as you begin to assess if you're being present, you're no longer being present.

- Triggers such as comparison, past trauma, and communication challenges can stop you from being fully present. Utilizing mindfulness strategies can support you through these triggers.
- Do your best to prioritize self-care daily. Taking care of yourself emotionally, mentally, and physically is an integral part of learning to be present with your partner.

CHAPTER 6

BUILDING TRUST

When you think about trust within your relationship, what's the first thing that comes to mind? Many people think of trusting their partner—the belief that the other person won't mislead, betray, or let them down. Maybe you also consider trust in the future and longevity of your partnership. But what about trusting yourself? While a strong bond with your partner is vital for a thriving relationship, this chapter delves into something even more essential: cultivating trust *within yourself.* No amount of trust in, or from, your partner can replace a void of self-trust.

Building external trust in relationships actually begins from within. This chapter will show you how to nurture confidence in your own resilience, capabilities, and innate worthiness. By increasing self-confidence, you'll gain the ability to manage waves of discomfort and uncertainty, knowing you can find solid ground even when the world around you shifts. You will learn that trust in your relationship is less about knowing everything will work out the way you hope it will and more about knowing you will be okay even if it doesn't.

SELF-TRUST

Self-trust is the act of having a fundamental belief in your abilities, decisions, and worthiness. It is deeply rooted in a compassionate acceptance of both your strengths and your limitations. It is not about trusting you'll always make the "right" decision—it's about trusting you will be okay even if things don't go as planned. At its core, self-trust involves nurturing a sense of faith in yourself and encompasses having confidence in your ability to make choices aligned with your personal values and goals, as well as pivoting through setbacks and failures with grace and determination.

Self-trust also entails honoring your needs and boundaries and acknowledging the importance of self-care and self-compassion during difficult times. When you trust yourself, you can create a foundation of inner security and emotional resilience, which can help foster personal growth. And when you feel that way inside, you are better able to foster healthy external relationships.

What Is Emotional Resilience?

Emotional resilience in the context of relationship anxiety means finding ways to bounce back from relationship challenges (including doubts or fears) by practicing coping strategies, seeking support, and showing yourself self-compassion. Building emotional resilience empowers you to face anxiety with courage, leading to a stronger connection with your partner.

Developing a strong sense of self-trust can also empower you to challenge the patterns of doubt and insecurity that fuel anxiety within your relationship. By cultivating self-trust, you gain greater confidence in your own judgment and capabilities, reducing your reliance on external validation or reassurance-seeking behaviors. For example, instead of seeking reassurance from your partner every time you feel insecure, self-trust allows you to self-soothe and reassure yourself independently.

THE POWER OF SELF-COMPASSION IN BUILDING SELF-TRUST

When life knocks you to the ground, do you extend a helping hand or kick yourself while you're down? Having self-compassion is like choosing to extend yourself that helping hand. Self-compassion is the practice of treating yourself with kindness, understanding, and acceptance, particularly in difficult moments. It involves extending the same empathy to yourself that you would offer to a loved one. When you show yourself compassion, you acknowledge your humanity, imperfections, and struggles without judgment or self-criticism.

Showing Self-Compassion Does Not Mean Lowering Your Standards

For those of you with exceptionally high standards, don't worry—being kind to yourself does not decrease your drive, standards, or expectations! Being compassionate with yourself isn't about letting yourself off the hook, making excuses for your actions or behaviors, or going "soft." It's about treating yourself with loving-kindness while still holding yourself accountable for growth. It's about being proud of and gentle toward yourself as you work toward achieving your next goal.

Practicing Self-Compassion Yields Benefits

Practicing self-compassion is the foundation to learning, growing, and healing by showing yourself kindness rather than criticism. It is linked to greater emotional resilience, reduced levels of anxiety and depression, and improved overall well-being. Kristin Neff, PhD, a pioneer in the field of self-compassion, has consistently concluded through her research that when you treat yourself with kindness and understanding, you can better manage your emotions and navigate life's ups and downs.

A part of learning to trust yourself involves acknowledging your limitations and imperfections. This can sometimes trigger feelings of shame or frustration, which leads to self-criticism. But self-compassion can serve as a beautiful antidote to shame because it helps quiet the critical voices in your head.

Self-Compassion Plays a Role in Managing Relationship Anxiety

Embracing self-compassion as you work to overcome relationship anxiety can lead to quicker, stronger, and better results because it:

- Discourages critical self-talk.
- Enables you to accept life's normal uncertainties.
- Promotes healthier communication patterns.

The more deeply you lean in to treating yourself with kindness and understanding, the more deeply you can develop a sense of self-trust and ultimately more relationship satisfaction.

Self-compassion also encourages you to treat yourself with the same love, respect, and understanding you want from your partner, especially during difficult times. Remember, if you can't give something to yourself, your brain will struggle to believe you deserve to receive it from your partner or anyone else. Since your brain tends to reinforce what it believes to be true, if it thinks you're unworthy of your own kindness and forgiveness, it'll continue to berate you, reject kindness and forgiveness from your partner, and perpetuate the belief that perfection is necessary for relationship success.

How to Practice Self-Compassion

If you've spent years shaming and blaming yourself, practicing self-compassion might feel foreign—or even impossible—at first. But like any skill, it's something you can learn and refine over time, and it's imperative to practice it on a daily basis, especially at first. It is not something to dabble in from time to time but rather something to incorporate into your everyday routine. Here are some ways you can integrate self-compassion into your daily life:

- **Speak to yourself as you would a child or close friend:** Use gentle and encouraging language when addressing yourself, especially during difficult moments.

- **Swap judgmental words and phrases for gentler language:** Replace self-criticism with words of support and understanding. For example: A "before" statement might sound like "I always ruin things with my insecurities; I'm so annoying" and the "after" statement like "It's okay to feel insecure sometimes; I am working on understanding and managing my feelings."
- **Keep a gratitude or celebration journal:** Take time each day to reflect on things you're grateful for or moments of achievement—no matter how small!
- **Be patient with yourself:** Allow yourself the time and space to grow and learn, and recognize that progress takes time.
- **Remind yourself that you are a flawed human, like everyone else:** Do your best to embrace your imperfections as part of what makes you uniquely human.
- **Practice self-forgiveness:** Try to let go of past mistakes and treat yourself with the same forgiveness you would extend to others.
- **Comfort your body:** Physical touch, like a hug, massage, or foot rub, can be a powerful way to soothe and comfort yourself during challenging times.
- **Nurture your body:** Nourish your body with food, time in nature, or rest.
- **Set encouraging reminders on your phone:** Use technology to remind yourself to practice self-compassion regularly—set up reminders with motivational messages to pop up on your devices each day.
- **Write yourself supportive notes:** Surround yourself with reminders of your worth and capability by placing supportive messages on sticky notes on your mirror or around your house.

If you can integrate one or more of these practices into your daily life, you will cultivate a deeper sense of self-compassion and reap the benefits of greater emotional resilience, reduced anxiety, and stronger self-trust.

When You Are Kind to Yourself,
You're More Likely to Trust Yourself

Self-compassion lays the foundation for understanding and accepting yourself with kindness—and it also opens the door to fostering deeper trust in your own capabilities, resourcefulness, and worthiness. In comparison to those driven by self-criticism or perfectionism, people with a strong sense of self-compassion are more likely to pursue bigger goals with greater enthusiasm. Compassionate self-awareness not only strengthens your internal sense of trust, but it also reduces the barriers that hinder your ability to trust yourself fully.

5 ESSENTIAL TYPES OF SELF-TRUST FOR HEALTHY RELATIONSHIPS

There are five key elements that can help you deepen self-trust in relationships. They are:

- Trust that you are capable.
- Trust that you are resourceful.
- Trust that you will be okay.
- Trust that you are worthy.
- Trust that your relationship can withstand hardship.

Building confidence in each of these categories will provide you with the assurance needed to embrace the ups and downs that come with all relationships.

Trust That You Are Capable

It's so important that you celebrate your inner strength and capability as you learn to trust yourself. It's easy to underestimate yourself, especially when you're constantly faced with the many uncertainties and challenges that come with being in a relationship. However, by embracing the concept of self-efficacy, you can begin to harness the power you possess to handle challenges with strength and confidence.

What Is Self-Efficacy?

Self-efficacy, as described by psychologist Albert Bandura, PhD, refers to your belief in your ability to accomplish tasks and achieve goals. It's essentially trusting that you possess the skills and resilience necessary to thrive and overcome obstacles, regardless of what the future has in store for you. In the context of relationships, self-efficacy refers to the belief in your capacity to:

- Communicate effectively.
- Resolve conflicts constructively.
- Accept moments of uncertainty and disconnection.
- Successfully move forward if your relationship doesn't turn out the way you hoped.

Many of us harbor limiting beliefs or self-doubts about our abilities within relationships. You might question whether you're good enough, whether you have what it takes to make the relationship work, or whether you deserve love and happiness. On the other end of the spectrum, you might doubt whether your partner is good enough, whether they have what it takes to make a relationship work, or whether they're deserving enough of your love and generosity. Regardless of where you fall on this spectrum, when it comes to relationship anxiety, these beliefs often stem from fear and insecurity rather than reality. When you start challenging these limiting beliefs and reframing them in a more empowering light, you will begin to increase your self-efficacy.

People with low self-efficacy for accomplishing a specific task are more likely to avoid it or try to control the outcome. Those who believe they are capable are more likely to wholeheartedly participate in a task without focusing on the outcome. For example:

- If you believe you cannot bounce back from conflict with your partner, you might not voice your opinion or concerns in hopes of avoiding conflict.
  - …But if you are confident in your ability to navigate conflict, you will be more willing to communicate openly about your opinions and concerns, which can lead to healthier communication, deeper connection, and a stronger partnership.
- If you believe you must know for sure if your partner is "The One," you are likely to continuously judge, analyze, and test them in hopes of avoiding uncertainty.
  - …But if you are confident in your ability to have a fulfilling life with a partner without knowing for sure if they're "The One," you will be more willing to be present and vulnerable, leading to greater relationship satisfaction.
- If you believe you could never survive a breakup, you might be hesitant to commit fully to a relationship in the first place.
  - …But if you trust that you are capable of navigating a season of heartache (though of course no one wants that), you will be more willing to fully commit to the relationship in the here and now.

These examples show how trusting in your capabilities offers you more freedom to be open, present, and confident in your relationship.

How Do You Cultivate Self-Efficacy?

If you notice yourself doubting your capabilities, try not to be discouraged. One way to increase self-efficacy is to remind yourself that you already have it! Reflect on past experiences where you have successfully navigated challenges or overcome obstacles you thought you wouldn't be able to. Perhaps you've effectively communicated your needs to your partner, resolved a disagreement with grace and understanding, or supported each other through a difficult time. These experiences serve as evidence that you're capable of overcoming challenges and should give you a boost of optimism and motivation.

Additional strategies for cultivating self-efficacy include:

- **Identifying and reframing limiting beliefs:** Be mindful of the stories you tell yourself on a regular basis. Are they helping you feel more or less capable? Are they rooted in fact or fear? Be sure you're rooting *for*, not *against*, yourself. For example, "I'll never be good at communicating my needs effectively so I shouldn't even try" could be reframed as "Learning to communicate effectively takes practice, and I'm better at communicating now than I used to be."
- **Setting achievable goals:** Break down larger goals into smaller, more manageable tasks. Start by finishing easy tasks and gradually move up to tackling ones that are slightly outside your comfort zone but still within your reach. As you successfully complete these, your confidence in your abilities will grow, increasing self-efficacy and self-trust.
- **Embracing failure:** Do your best to view failure as part of the process. Think of it as a stepping stone along the path to success rather than evidence of your inability to succeed.
- **Practicing self-compassion:** When you face setbacks or challenges, respond to yourself with kindness and understanding rather than self-criticism. As discussed earlier in this chapter, cultivating self-compassion is essential for nurturing self-confidence and self-efficacy.

Incorporating these additional strategies into your daily routine will give you the best chance at cultivating a stronger sense of self-efficacy and strengthening your sense of self-trust.

Trust That You Are Resourceful

Trusting yourself in a relationship often involves navigating uncertainty and taking steps without fully knowing the outcome. It's natural to feel overwhelmed when faced with a complex task, especially when you don't know exactly what to expect. Imagine the process of assembling a piece of furniture. You start with a large pile of parts and hardware that looks like it's never going to become a shelf. At first glance, it might seem impossible, and you might feel defeated before even getting started. However, as you follow the instructions step by step, the process becomes clearer. While you might not be able to envision step 12 when you're on step 1, once you get to step 11, the resources you'll need for step 12 become clearer.

Similarly, trusting yourself in a relationship means taking things one step at a time, even when the path ahead seems uncertain. You may not have all the answers from the beginning, but by trusting in your resourcefulness, you can have faith in your ability to tackle challenges as they arise. As with assembling furniture, each step in your relationship journey builds on the last, leading to a clearer understanding of what to do next.

When navigating relationship challenges, it's helpful to tap into both your inner and your external resources for support. Your inner resources include qualities such as resilience, creativity, adaptability, and problem-solving skills. These are the innate tools you carry within yourself that are available to you at any time. You can probably think of times in your life when you've already utilized these tools. Maybe you've demonstrated resilience in the face of adversity or found creative solutions to an unforeseen problem.

In addition to your inner resources, external support can also be helpful when encountering obstacles within your relationship. This may involve seeking guidance from trusted friends, family members, mentors, therapists, or coaches, who can offer valuable perspectives and recommendations. Just as you might consult the instruction manual or grab necessary tools when assembling furniture, looking for support and guidance can provide you with the resources you need in a relationship too.

Trusting in your resourcefulness also involves embracing flexibility and adaptability in the face of uncertainty. Relationships, like most areas of life, are inherently unpredictable, and issues often arise when you least expect them. By embracing a mindset that's open to change and being willing to adapt to new circumstances, you will be more confident you have the tools you need to deal with these unexpected situations.

Trust That You Will Be Okay

You wouldn't be where you are today if you hadn't already weathered some storms. The very fact that you're reading this book serves as evidence of your resilience and resourcefulness. But being resilient doesn't mean you're immune to pain; nobody is.

It's understandable to have thoughts like "How would I ever survive that?" or "I don't have what it takes to make it through something like that." Thoughts like these stem from both limiting beliefs and a natural instinct for self-protection. Your mind is wired to anticipate and avoid potential threats, and believing that you could never handle something is your brain's way of trying to shield you from harm. However, this protective mechanism often leads to avoidance, which as you know from Chapter 3, keeps you stuck rather than helping you grow.

When you acknowledge that these thoughts are rooted in a desire for self-preservation, you can begin to understand that they're valid… but not necessarily reflective of reality. Instead, they represent your mind's attempt to keep you safe by discouraging you from stepping outside your comfort zone. While that may feel comfortable in the short term, long-term growth requires confronting challenges and overcoming obstacles, even when they seem daunting at first.

Part of cultivating self-trust is trusting that the version of yourself you need to be will emerge the moment it needs to. Even if you can't yet imagine how you'll make it through a difficult situation, trust that you will figure it out if/when the time comes.

There is no doubt you've already overcome numerous obstacles in life you once thought insurmountable. You are capable. You are resourceful. You will figure things out, and you will be okay.

Pain Is Part of the Human Experience

That said, being "okay" doesn't mean you'll never experience pain, disappointment, or heartache. It just means you'll learn to navigate these challenges and emotions. You'll grieve, grow, and adapt. Each experience, whether positive or negative, shapes you and contributes to who you are today.

Trusting that you will be okay is not about minimizing fears or feelings; it's about recognizing them but pushing forward using your own resilience and strength. When you trust that you will be okay regardless of the outcome, the outcome itself becomes less daunting and worrisome. This shift allows you to focus on being present in the moment rather than worrying about what might happen in the future.

Trust That You Are Worthy

Trusting that you are lovable and worthy of a healthy and happy relationship is another essential aspect under the bigger umbrella of self-trust. Your sense of worthiness shapes how you perceive and interact with your partner. Harboring doubts about whether or not you deserve a great relationship makes it challenging to accept that you're in a great relationship, even when it's right in front of you. Trusting that you are worthy means acknowledging your inherent value and embracing the belief that you deserve love, intimacy, and emotional fulfillment. Remind yourself that:

- You deserve to be heard, have needs, and assert your boundaries within a relationship.
- Your needs, desires, and aspirations are equally as valid and significant as your partner's.

Accepting these truths forms the foundation for balanced relationship dynamics.

Part of owning your worth involves knowing it does not change, regardless of any heartache or trauma you've experienced. Your past does not define your present, nor does it dictate your future capacity for love and connection. Trusting that you can open your heart to love, even if you've been hurt or disappointed in the past, can help release limiting beliefs that may be holding you back. Vulnerability is not a sign of weakness but a courageous act of self-approval and authenticity. By embracing vulnerability, you create space for genuine connection and intimacy to grow within your relationship.

When you trust your worthiness, you know you have nothing to prove to others. You are worthy of what you want in your relationships without having to convince anyone else of your deservingness. Trust in what *you* know to be true within your partnership, regardless of others' opinions or judgments. While support from friends and family can feel good, your worth stands on its own, independent of external validation or approval.

As you trust that you are lovable and deserving of a deeply connected relationship, you will become more empowered to embrace love with confidence and authenticity. Trusting that you are worthy of great things in your relationship opens up space for you to receive great things in your relationship. The more you believe in your inherent worth, the safer your body will feel experiencing joy and love.

> Case Study: Deserving of Love

Despite their being together for three years, Maya's self-doubt often strained her relationship with Antonio. She struggled with feelings of unworthiness and constantly questioned whether she deserved his love and whether she was good enough for him.

These doubts over her worthiness often manifested in her testing Antonio's love for her and seesawing between being affectionate and being distant. This behavior frequently led to misunderstandings and conflicts between them. Maya's fear of not being worthy of love made it difficult for her to fully trust in the depth of Antonio's feelings for her.

Antonio, sensing Maya's insecurities but unsure how to help her overcome them, felt frustrated and helpless at times. He wished that Maya could see herself as he saw her: worthy, lovable, and deserving of happiness.

Maya began to realize that her attempts to test Antonio's love weren't helping her feel more secure; they were actually making her feel even *less* worthy and were pushing him away. Determined to show up differently, Maya began to reframe the negative beliefs she had about herself and cultivate a practice of self-compassion and self-trust. She started embracing the fact that she was, and always had been, "good enough" for love.

As Maya started to trust in her own worthiness, she noticed a shift in her relationship. She stopped testing Antonio's love and dismissing his affection. Her increased willingness to give and receive love not only strengthened her own confidence but also brought them closer as a couple.

Trust That Your Relationship Can Withstand Hardship

Trusting that your partnership can withstand conflict and hardship is not just about having baseless faith; it's about recognizing the strength and commitment in your bond. While it's common to feel anxious when you're faced with disagreements or challenges, it's essential to have trust in the foundation of your relationship.

Conflict is a natural part of any relationship. Instead of viewing conflict as a threat to the stability of your relationship, try to view it as an opportunity for growth and deeper connection. Remember, it's not the absence of conflict that defines a healthy relationship—it's how you work through it together that matters.

While your anxious brain may attempt to tell you otherwise, it's crucial to remind yourself that not every argument or disagreement is a sign of impending doom for your relationship. Healthy relationships are built on a solid foundation of mutual respect, understanding, and trust—all qualities that can withstand the occasional rough patch. Trusting yourself and your partner means having faith in your ability to overcome obstacles together.

Building self-trust in relationships relies on trusting your judgment in choosing a partner who is committed to weathering the storms with you. Believe in your ability to settle with intention, knowing you've made a value-aligned choice with your partner. Trusting yourself in this way allows you to approach conflict with an open heart and a willingness to listen and understand each other's perspectives. When you're confident in your ability to choose a partner who values mutual growth and connection, it becomes easier to have confidence in your ability to face challenges together.

Exercise:
Reflecting on Past Triumphs

Take a moment to list ten things that at one point you thought you couldn't do or would never get through. These could include challenges you faced in relationships, personal goals you achieved, significant losses or health challenges you've endured, or obstacles you overcame in your professional or academic life.

Next, reflect on each item on your list and consider the emotions, thoughts, and challenges you experienced while overcoming them. How did you feel when faced with these obstacles? What thoughts or beliefs did you have about your ability to overcome them?

As you review your list, acknowledge the capability, resilience, and resourcefulness that allowed you to overcome these challenges. Recognize that each triumph, no matter how big or small, contributed to the person you are today. These past successes are a testament to your ability to overcome and persevere.

Lastly, consider how you can apply what you just discovered to your daily life and relationships. When you start to doubt yourself or face challenges in your relationship, revisit your list as a reminder of your inner strength and ability to overcome adversity. Let your past triumphs serve as a source of inspiration and empowerment as you continue to build self-trust and confidence in yourself and your relationships.

Key Takeaways

- Trusting yourself is fundamental to building trust within your relationship. Self-trust involves believing in your abilities, decisions, and worthiness and is strengthened through self-compassion and self-efficacy.
- Practicing self-compassion is vital for nurturing self-trust. When you treat yourself with kindness and understanding, especially during difficult times, you can reduce self-criticism, better accept uncertainty, promote healthier communication patterns, and encourage greater emotional resilience.
- You've already proven you can do it! Reflecting on past wins, both personally and in relationships, can help you recognize your capability, resilience, and resourcefulness. Each success, no matter how small, contributes to your growth and shapes who you are today.

CHAPTER 7

BEING CURIOUS INSTEAD OF JUDGMENTAL

How often have you created a story in your mind about what your partner thinks, wants, or feels without even asking them? We've all been there: jumping to conclusions, assuming the worst, and letting fear dictate our reactions. Unfortunately, attempting to read your partner's mind—or expecting them to read yours—rarely works. What assumptions do you find yourself making about your partner's behavior? How do these assumptions influence your feelings and actions? Do they typically make you feel better or worse about your partner, yourself, and your relationship?

More than likely, they make you feel worse. What if, instead of creating stories from a place of judgment, fear, or defensiveness, you paused to ask questions and seek understanding? You can unlock a lot of important information about yourself and your relationship by embracing a more curious mindset. This chapter will highlight how stepping back to see the bigger picture and cultivating curiosity can be powerful antidotes to anxiety, judgment, and catastrophizing. From examining your own assumptions to taking your partner's actions or inactions less personally, this chapter will teach you practical strategies to boost your curiosity.

GIVE YOURSELF PERMISSION TO CHANGE YOUR MIND

The best way to foster a curious mindset is to be open and willing to change your mind when presented with new information and perspectives. Remember, in part due to confirmation bias, your brain prefers the comfort of being right, which requires less effort than challenging your current beliefs. Overcoming this bias requires actively seeking alternative perspectives and points of view, even if that process makes you feel uncomfortable. Otherwise, your brain will cling to what's familiar. For those with relationship anxiety, what's familiar can often mean fixating on doubt and worst-case scenarios.

As you begin to embrace a more curious mindset, it may initially feel like a blow to both your anxiety and your ego. That's partly because as you create the space for multiple possibilities and explanations, you may recognize that you are in fact wrong about things you once thought you knew for sure.

Let Go of Your Ego

Granting yourself permission to change your mind based on new information is a positive sign of growth, maturity, and healing. However, it's not uncommon for your ego to interpret this as a negative.

After all, it can sting to learn you were wrong or hadn't considered a certain point of view. You may find yourself caught between wanting to dig in your heels for the sake of being right and to humbly pivot for the sake of being content and growing as a person. While it can feel uncomfortable in the moment, choosing to pivot will bring you more happiness and connection in your relationship long term.

Be Gentle with Yourself

When you find yourself presented with the opportunity to reconsider your perspective, it's crucial to be compassionate with yourself. While no one likes to be served a slice of humble pie, sometimes it's the most nourishing thing. In these moments, you have a choice: resist the new information due to fear of being wrong or embrace it as evidence of your emotional intelligence, adaptability, and dedication to building a healthy relationship.

What Is Emotional Intelligence?

Emotional intelligence is the ability to recognize, understand, and manage your own emotions, as well as to understand and empathize with the emotions of others. It involves self-awareness, self-regulation, social awareness, and relational skills. Emotional intelligence is essential for stress reduction, effective communication, decision-making, conflict resolution, and genuine connection.

Wear Shoes That Fit

Something that can help you practice self-compassion—encouraging you to remain open-minded—is to remind yourself that you've always done the best you could with the information, skills, and energy you had at the time. Whatever beliefs, stories, and coping mechanisms you're defaulting to served you at one time. Your brain and body were doing the best they could to protect you, and they did a great job—you're still here!

However, just because something once served you doesn't mean it still does. A size 1 shoe served you at some point but probably wouldn't be the best fit now. Granting yourself permission to change your mind is like granting yourself permission to buy a new pair of shoes rather than trying to force your now size 8 feet into a size 1 shoe. As you grow and circumstances change, it's healthy and expected to outgrow things that were once a great fit—including your beliefs and perspectives.

Stop Making Up Stories

Building trust in your partner and relationship involves releasing unfounded assumptions. It's common for those with relationship anxiety to cling to stories and ideas they don't even *want* to be true. For example, when you are driven by a desire to assert control and validate your fears, you might:

- Tell yourself that your partner secretly wants to be with someone else, just so you can feel vindicated if they leave you.

- Convince yourself that you can't trust anyone as a defense mechanism against possible future betrayals.
- Hesitate to share positive aspects of your relationship with friends to protect yourself from potential humiliation if it ends.

These stories are your brain's attempt to shield you from future hurt and betrayal, but ultimately they only cause you to hurt in the present. They're also examples of betting on the outcome you don't want, which is a common tendency among those with relationship anxiety, but it's a self-defeating strategy. Don't be more committed to what you *don't* want than to what you *do* want! Instead, prioritize what you truly desire.

Remember, your brain seeks evidence to validate your beliefs. If you convince yourself that your partner doesn't prioritize you, you'll only notice evidence that they don't prioritize you. However, by entertaining the possibility that your partner does prioritize you, you'll begin to notice evidence that they do. Embracing a curious mindset means granting yourself permission to release outdated beliefs. Even if those beliefs once provided a sense of protection, they now restrict you. Grant yourself permission to risk being wrong about your partner, and be open to beliefs and ideas that would better serve your relationship today.

AVOID MAKING ASSUMPTIONS

Your mind is capable of generating elaborate narratives based on assumptions rather than facts. With a heightened sensitivity to fear and uncertainty, those with relationship anxiety are particularly prone to making assumptions. Though it's possible to make both positive and negative assumptions, anxiety often skews you toward negative ones. Consequently, rather than assuming best-case scenarios, it's more likely you interpret situations in a negative light, assume worst-case scenarios, and preemptively seek solutions to problems that have not yet occurred.

In relationships, assumptions manifest as ingrained beliefs, expectations, or interpretations about yourself, your partner, or the relationship as a whole that you accept as truth without sufficient evidence. For example, you may immediately assume that your partner's delayed response to a text message signifies they are disinterested or out cheating on you. In reality, the delay could be something innocuous, such as they got caught up at work or their phone battery died. Despite the delay being innocent, your initial assumption may lead to feelings of insecurity, resentment, or mistrust, which causes unnecessary anxiety and strains the relationship.

Human nature craves certainty, especially in relationships. If you're grappling with relationship anxiety, this craving intensifies, leading to a reliance on assumptions to fill the void of uncertainty. Rather than facing the discomfort of not knowing or the vulnerability in communicating with your partner, relying on assumptions offers a false sense of security. Playing off your ideas, fears, and beliefs, your imagination will invent an explanation. Believing this explanation, even if incorrect, somehow feels better than being uncertain.

Common Assumptions in Relationships

Assumptions—which can be influenced by fear, past experiences, societal norms, and personal insecurities—can significantly shape your thoughts, perceptions, and behaviors within your relationship. If you are able to challenge these assumptions with curiosity, you are more likely to dispense with false stories and replace them with a realistic outlook. Let's explore some of the ways assumptions can show up in your relationship dynamics:

- **Assuming intention:** This can look like assuming that your partner's words and actions have negative intentions, such as assuming they bought you flowers only because they did something wrong. Or it could be assuming your partner is doing something with ulterior motives, such as showing you affection not because they care about you but because they want to have sex.

- **Assuming responsibility:** Assuming responsibility for your partner's emotions or actions can look like presuming that something you did caused their anger or sadness (or vice versa).
- **Assuming control:** Assuming that you can control or change your partner's behavior or feelings is another way assumptions can show up. For example, you might assume that you can make them love you more by being more accommodating or by having fewer needs.
- **Assuming feelings:** Trying to read your partner's mind without asking them directly and know what they are feeling without them telling you means you're assuming feelings. For example, you might assume they're upset with you because they're quiet.
- **Assuming understanding or lack thereof:** Here you're assuming that your partner understands your thoughts or feelings without you expressing them directly. For example, you might assume they know when you're upset or need support without you explicitly saying that. Or maybe you assume that your partner will never understand how you're feeling, so you don't even try to communicate with them.
- **Assuming stagnation:** Stagnation is assuming that the way the relationship is currently is the way it will always be, positive or negative. This may show up as assuming that because you're in a state of infatuation, you'll always feel that way or that because you're in a rut, you'll be in a rut indefinitely.
- **Assuming future outcomes:** You might assume that a conflict or disagreement will inevitably lead to the end of the relationship, such as guessing that your partner will leave you if you disagree with their opinion on something.

- **Assuming perfection:** This looks like believing that your partner should *always* show up as the best and highest version of themselves. For example, you might expect they'll *always* be upbeat and happy around your friends.

- **Assuming compatibility or incompatibility:** If you assume that similarities (or differences) in opinions, interests, or values automatically indicate compatibility (or incompatibility), you are closing off natural differences that can still be present in a great relationship. Your preference for tropical vacations and your partner's preference for the snowy mountains doesn't automatically make you both incompatible.

- **Assuming untrustworthiness:** Assuming untrustworthiness is the process of guessing that your partner is untrustworthy or will be deceitful based on past experiences or insecurities, such as assuming your current partner will betray you because a past partner did.

- **Assuming rejection or abandonment:** If you are afraid that expressing vulnerability or emotional needs will lead to rejection or abandonment, you are assuming your partner will leave you if they knew the "real you."

- **Assuming helplessness:** Operating under the assumption that you are not capable enough to cope with challenges or setbacks in the relationship is a false helplessness. This can also look like assuming that you could never have a full and enjoyable life without a partner and/or that you would never survive a breakup or rejection.

- **Assuming independence:** If you assume independence, you believe you can never fully count on anyone and it's only a matter of time before they let you down, so you don't want to become too vulnerable or dependent on them. This may manifest as choosing not to date, refusing to commit to anything long term, or believing you don't "need" anyone.

- **Assuming self-worth:** Assuming that your worth, beauty, happiness, and value are based on your partner choosing you, validating you, and approving of you is another problematic assumption. For example, you might believe that if your partner criticizes a choice or behavior, you are less than, unworthy, or unlovable.
- **Assuming brokenness:** If the relationship doesn't work out for any reason, you might assume it is because you are irrevocably flawed or broken and therefore not good enough or lovable enough to sustain a healthy partnership.

As you can see based on how long that list was, assumptions can—and do—show up just about anywhere! If you see yourself reflected in several of these examples, try not to be discouraged. Assuming, like so many other behaviors, is a learned behavior. It's something your brain has adopted at some point as a means of self-protection and survival, but you do have the power to change it.

Assumptions Don't Actually Protect You from Discomfort

Interestingly, many people *assume* that making assumptions about their partner's thoughts, feelings, or behaviors will protect them from abandonment, rejection, humiliation, or being blindsided. There is often an underlying (faulty) belief that you can stay one step ahead by assuming everything your partner is thinking, feeling, and doing. And if you can stay a step ahead, you think you can prepare.

For instance, if you assume that your partner will be upset if you disagree with them, you can agree with them on everything. If you assume that your partner is going to break up with you, you can break up with them first. If you assume that your partner will be unfaithful, you can say, "I told you so" if it happens. A major flaw in this process, however, is that assuming the worst doesn't really protect you from future pain. It only robs you from present peace. As such, one way to return to a place of peace is to practice taking things less personally.

OVERCOMING RELATIONSHIP ANXIETY

TRY NOT TO TAKE EVERYTHING PERSONALLY

Taking things personally is another common way people make assumptions. Assuming everything revolves around you is draining and creates a one-sided conversation that neglects the true complexity of relationships. It's essential to recognize that not everything your partner does is a reflection of you or your relationship. While you certainly should play a significant role in your partner's life, it's important to acknowledge that you're not the center of every action or decision your partner makes. Just as you have your individuality within the relationship, so do they.

Curiosity can help you detach and depersonalize your partner's actions, because it encourages you to look for deeper understanding and connection. When you assume you already know something, there's little room for curiosity or growth. Your beliefs dictate your reactions, and limiting beliefs can lead to misunderstandings and conflict. When you let go of preconceived notions and remain open to new knowledge, you empower yourself to respond to your partner and relationship with more grace and authenticity.

HOW TO DEAL WITH "THE ICK"

Social media has brought to light a phenomenon related to judgment that you may have heard of: "the ick." While not a new concept, social media has popularized it, shining a spotlight on those moments when you suddenly feel repulsed or disgusted by your partner, usually because of a specific behavior. This behavior can range from a trivial annoyance, like snorting when laughing or wearing socks to bed, to a more significant concern, such as being rude to waitstaff or displaying self-centered behavior. The experience of "the ick" can elicit a strong visceral reaction and may lead you to question the viability of your relationship.

For those grappling with relationship anxiety, experiencing "the ick" can exacerbate distress. You might find yourself wondering, "Is this a genuine red flag, or is it my anxiety amplifying minor issues?" In such moments, it's helpful to revisit your values, needs, and relationship vision. Is the behavior in question a fundamental value mismatch or a boundary violation, or is it simply a harmless turnoff? Can you communicate your preferences with your partner and work together on a resolution? Is it a quirk you can learn to accept despite not particularly liking it?

When "the ick" arises from preferences rather than red flags, practicing acceptance and tolerating discomfort can be beneficial. Recognize that you're not expected to love or be attracted to everything your partner does. There may be things your partner does that you'd rather they didn't, and that's okay. While assessing the overall health of your relationship, if you find yourself fixating on minor irritations despite genuinely loving your partner, it's more likely relationship anxiety at play opposed to a genuine red flag.

However, there are instances when "the ick" could be a valid indication to reconsider the relationship. For example, if you dread spending time with your partner, don't want any physical contact with them, or can't envision a future with this person because their behavior clearly conflicts with your values, it is time to reassess. While chemistry doesn't need to be instantaneous, ongoing feelings of irritation, disgust, or fear for your well-being are pretty clear signs this person isn't right for you.

Remember, there's a distinction between being turned off by true red flags and being turned off by human imperfections. While some instances of "the ick" may signal deeper issues, often it's about accepting certain quirks or habits as part of the package deal of a real relationship. In these cases, it's on you to navigate and overcome these minor aversions rather than expecting your partner to change every aspect of who they are. By fostering open communication and maintaining realistic expectations, you can learn to be more flexible and accepting of your partner's perceived flaws.

HOW TO BECOME MORE CURIOUS

Becoming curious requires you to challenge your immediate assumptions and open up space for alternative explanations. It's learning that your initial assumption can be *one* possible explanation but not necessarily the *only* explanation. Becoming curious allows you to entertain your assumption as one possibility rather than automatically accepting it as the truth. While sometimes your assumption is correct, many times it is not. Becoming curious and recognizing there are multiple possibilities can minimize how often you feel defensive and/or fall into catastrophizing. Becoming more curious can also help you both decrease feelings of judgment and increase understanding of your partner.

One of the simplest ways to begin to introduce more curiosity in the face of assumptions is to ask yourself: "I wonder why…?"; "I wonder how…?"; or "I wonder what…?" Revisiting some of the assumptions we discussed earlier in this chapter, here are a few examples of how you could introduce these new phrases:

Assuming Intention
- Event: Your partner buys you flowers.
- Assumption: They must've done something wrong.
- Curiosity: I wonder why they bought me flowers today.
- Possibilities: They did something "wrong"....*Or* They love me; they were thinking of me; they know I enjoy thoughtful surprises; they know how loved I felt last time I got flowers; the shop was having a sale on my favorite flowers.

Assuming Feelings
- Event: Your partner is more quiet than usual.
- Assumption: They're upset with me.
- Curiosity: I wonder why they're quiet today.
- Possibilities: They are upset with me....*Or* They're feeling under the weather; they didn't sleep well last night; their social battery

is drained from a challenging day at work; they are worried about a friend who's going through a hard time; they feel safe and secure in my presence without the pressure to have to talk; they are in a bad mood and don't want to say something they might regret.

Assuming Helplessness
- Event: My partner and I break up.
- Assumption: I will never get over it.
- Curiosity: I wonder how I'll move forward now that we've broken up.
- Possibilities: I will never get over it....*Or* I will grieve; I will find a support system; I will explore new hobbies I've been putting off while in partnership; I will see how capable I am of living with hurt and disappointment; I will gain clarity on my values and nonnegotiables for future relationships.

These scenarios show how curiosity can prompt you to uncover alternative perspectives and challenge your initial assumptions, as well as give you the opportunity to learn something new about your partner. The possibility of learning more about your partner can motivate you to communicate with them rather than spiraling or shutting down.

RELEASING JUDGMENT

When you're wrestling with relationship anxiety, it's uncommon to jump to positive conclusions. Typically, making assumptions involves negative judgment: of yourself, your partner, or both. This is where curiosity becomes particularly valuable—it encourages you to view experiences through a more neutral lens and to approach situations with genuine inquisitiveness instead of snap judgment.

For instance, imagine a scenario where you're feeling anxious and your partner doesn't offer you support or reassurance. At this point, judgment may kick in, telling you that your partner is unsupportive. You may view this situation as proof they're not the one for you, they don't love you, or you're incapable of finding a supportive partner. However, in this state of discomfort, it's important to recognize that such judgments may not necessarily be true.

Truly embracing curiosity in this situation involves asking questions like: "I wonder why they are not supportive when I'm feeling anxious? Is that out of character for them? Have I ever communicated my struggles with anxiety to them? Have I accepted their support in the past when it was offered?" Digging deeper to answer these questions moves you away from judgment and into curiosity and connection.

Judgment Leads to Miscommunication and Defensiveness

Perhaps your partner's lack of support does stem from carelessness or selfishness. Or maybe it's because they are unaware you are feeling anxious, as you might effectively hide it. Perhaps they have attempted to provide support in the past, only for it to be refused, leading them to believe you prefer to be left alone. Perhaps their way of coping with anxiety (space and quiet) might differ from yours (a hug), but they're assuming it's the same.

When judgment takes over, defensiveness often follows. This can lead to viewing your partner as an opponent rather than a teammate. It's challenging to maintain feelings of connection, safety, and joy when you see your partner as an enemy. Curiosity invites you to set aside judgment—both of your partner and of yourself—and encourages collaborative problem-solving. Bringing neutrality to a situation creates space in your mind to remember that your partner is your teammate and that it's safe to put away your armor.

It's also essential to recognize that not everyone thinks, acts, or reacts in the same way you do. Your partner's responses may differ from how you would respond in the same situation. Not everything obvious to you is obvious to your partner, and vice versa. Without effective, vulnerable communication, it's easy to judge yourself or your partner for actions or inactions. However, taking the time to get curious about the truth behind your or your partner's actions may provide insight that is very different from your initial assumption. That's why you are more likely to find common ground with your partner if you use curiosity instead of judgment.

> Case Study: A Curious Connection

When thirty-six-year-old Carmen first met thirty-three-year-old Louis, she was horrified to learn that he lived with his mother. Immediately, she found herself making assumptions about his character—that he was lacking ambition and unsuccessful. She couldn't understand why a grown man would still be living at home.

However, instead of writing him off based on her initial judgments, Carmen decided to approach the situation with curiosity. She asked Louis about his living arrangement, genuinely interested in understanding his perspective. To her surprise, Louis shared that he was living with his mom because she had been diagnosed with early-onset Alzheimer's disease. Louis was dedicating his time and energy to caring for his mom during this difficult time.

This new information completely shifted Carmen's perception of Louis. She realized that his decision to live at home was a testament to his compassion, family-oriented values, and kindness, not laziness or lack of motivation. His willingness to prioritize his mother's well-being highlighted qualities that Carmen deeply admired in a partner, not qualities she viewed as negatives.

By choosing curiosity over judgment, Carmen not only debunked her initial assumptions but also gained a deeper understanding of Louis's character. Their conversation brought them closer together and opened the door to further discussions about their values, priorities, and aspirations, strengthening their connection and laying the foundation for a meaningful relationship.

USE CURIOUS COMMUNICATION TO GET TO KNOW YOUR PARTNER MORE DEEPLY

Taking a moment to get genuinely curious about why your partner may act or feel a certain way can be transformative. That involves asking questions and using open communication to show genuine, judgment-free interest. Curious communication can use phrases such as *Tell me more about...*, *I'm interested in hearing your thoughts on...*, *I'd love to learn more about...*, or *Can you help me understand why...*? This approach encourages your partner to open up and share their thoughts and feelings without fear of judgment. For instance:

- If your partner is cautious with spending, you might assume they are not generous. With curious communication such as "I'm interested in hearing more about why you don't like to spend money on going out to eat," you may realize that they are saving for a future goal within the relationship, like a ring or a house.
- If your partner doesn't want you to meet their family early on in the relationship, you may assume they're ashamed of you or don't think you're good enough for their family. With curious communication such as "I'd love to learn more about your family," you may learn that they had a difficult childhood and remain distant from their family to protect their own mental health.
- Your partner may share details about your relationship with their family or friends, and you might assume they don't respect or protect your privacy. With curious communication such as "Can you help me understand why you shared those personal details with your family?" you may learn that they grew up in a family with different boundaries around sharing and didn't realize that you considered what they shared to be oversharing.
- If your partner consistently resists the idea of going out of town with you, you might assume they don't prioritize spending

quality time together. With curious communication such as "I'd love to learn more about why you're resistant to going out of town," you may learn that the thought of leaving their pets behind triggers a deep fear of loss and death.

- If your partner doesn't often initiate sex, you may assume they're not sexually attracted to you. Curious communication such as "Can you help me understand why you rarely initiate sex?" may reveal they have performance anxiety, sexual trauma, or deep insecurity about their own body.
- If your partner is continuously late to commitments, you might assume they don't value you or your time. Through curious communication such as "I'm interested in learning more about why being punctual is a struggle for you," you might learn that they have ADHD and struggle with managing their time.

These examples show how curious communication can help you gain more information instead of relying on judgments or assumptions. Even if the information you learn is hurtful or indicates that you and your partner don't have the same values, the process is still useful. Curious communication fosters empathy and provides either an opportunity for collaborative problem solving or more clarity on the fact that the relationship isn't a good fit.

ZOOM OUT FOR THE BEST PERSPECTIVE

It can be tempting to fixate on and analyze each action, inaction, thought, or behavior in your relationship, but continuously assessing your compatibility with your partner based on every single interaction can lead to misunderstanding and unnecessary conflict. This is where zooming out can be especially helpful.

Did your partner say something insensitive once? That might not mean the relationship is doomed. Does your partner zone out and forget what you say occasionally? It could be something to work on but doesn't necessarily mean they don't care about what you have to say.

Rather than judging and rejudging your compatibility based on each isolated interaction, take a step back. Observing trends and patterns over time allows you to more accurately identify areas of strength and areas for improvement. As you broaden your perspective, get curious: Is this something your partner does all the time or occasionally or rarely?

Instead of fixating on a single incident or conflict, reflect on the broader narrative of your relationship over the past week, month, or year. What you could assume to be a significant incompatibility in the moment might actually pale in comparison to the overall harmony and compatibility you experience together.

WHEN TO BE CAREFUL WITH CURIOSITY

While curiosity can be a powerful tool for deepening understanding and connection, it's important to recognize its boundaries, especially when it comes to relationship anxiety. Genuine curiosity stems from a desire to understand and empathize, not from an urgent need to know. When your anxiety takes over, sometimes controlling or compulsive behaviors can mask as "being curious."

Curiosity vs. Control

Being curious involves opening the door to deeper understanding through a collaborative dialogue, not intrusive questioning. Being curious about your partner is never about overstepping their boundaries or invading their privacy. Everyone has a right to personal space and autonomy, and it's essential to respect those boundaries even when you're curious about aspects of their life. Persuading your partner to share something with you because you're "curious" is not healthy curiosity; it is a form of controlling behavior. Healthy relationships thrive on mutual trust, and violating those boundaries can erode that trust.

As such, it's important to ensure that the motivation behind your curiosity is respectful and value aligned.

Curiosity vs. Reassurance Seeking

Additionally, using curiosity as a means of seeking reassurance or alleviating anxiety can also be problematic. That might sound like "I'm just curious if you still love me as much as you did when we first met" or "I'm just curious if you ever doubt our connection." While it's completely normal to seek comfort and validation from your partner from time to time, if you notice you're using "curiosity" as a way to temporarily relieve your anxiety, it's likely compulsive behavior, not genuine curiosity. As you recover from relationship anxiety, it is probably better for you to embrace the discomfort of not knowing and engage in positive self-care, not seek answers from your partner.

Curiosity can be a valuable asset in nurturing healthy relationships—when used as a way to challenge assumptions, reduce judgment, and understand your partner more deeply. By respecting boundaries, avoiding the temptation to seek reassurance compulsively, and prioritizing consent, you can harness the power of curiosity in a healthy way that benefits both you and your partner.

Exercise:
The What-If Spectrum

Your brain is great at coming up with what-ifs, but most of the time they're working against you. In this exercise, you'll challenge these automatic negative thoughts and assumptions by exploring a variety of possibilities along the what-if spectrum. Follow these steps:

1. **Identify your what-if thoughts:** Write about some recent moments when you caught yourself thinking in terms of what-if scenarios. For example, you might have thought, "What if my partner breaks up with me?"

2. **Create your what-if spectrum:** Divide a blank sheet of paper into two columns. Label one column "Current Assumptions" and the other "Alternative Perspectives." For each what-if thought you identify, challenge yourself to come up with alternative perspectives or possibilities. For example:

- Current: What if my partner breaks up with me?
- Alternative: What if my partner continues to cherish and support me throughout our relationship?

- Current: What if I don't really love my partner?
- Alternative: What if I can see a real possibility of a lasting future with my partner, and that's what scares me most because it feels so real and vulnerable?

3. **Hold space for both:** Reflect on how it feels to entertain positive, neutral, and negative what-if scenarios. Remind yourself that uncertainty is a natural part of life and that it's helpful to consider different outcomes before immediately jumping to conclusions.

4. **Keep a running list:** Keep your what-if spectrum handy and add to it whenever needed. Over time, you'll build a comprehensive list of possibilities, helping your brain remain curious and open-minded.

Key Takeaways

- By challenging assumptions and remaining open to multiple possibilities, you can minimize misunderstandings, decrease judgment, and build connection with your partner.
- Instead of jumping to conclusions or making assumptions, do your best to cultivate a mindset of curiosity. This involves being okay with changing your mind, questioning your initial

judgments, and seeking deeper understanding through entertaining alternative perspectives.

- Be mindful of passing unnecessary judgment. By letting go of preconceived notions and working toward taking things less personally, you can create more space for empathy and collaboration with your partner.

CHAPTER 8

SWAPPING FEAR-BASED DECISION-MAKING FOR VALUE-BASED DECISION-MAKING

Take a few minutes to recall the moments in your life that are tinged with regret. Were they aligned with your deepest values, or were they driven by fear and uncertainty? Probably the latter. Rarely do we look back and wish we hadn't pursued something that truly mattered to us at the time. Rarely do we regret following our truth or going after a meaningful dream, even if it led to challenges or uncertainties along the way. Instead, the times that bother us the most are when we ignored our instincts, succumbed to societal pressure, or let fear and anxiety dictate our decisions. As you reflect, you might find yourself wishing you had trusted yourself more, acted on your true desires, and cared less about external judgments and comparisons.

This chapter will focus on the concept of values—what they are, how they can guide you, and why they are essential in navigating relationship anxiety. By understanding and embracing your values, you can establish a reliable north star for decision-making, allowing you to steer away from fear-based living and toward a life aligned with what truly matters most to *you*. In doing so, you will learn how leaning into your values rather than your fears can unlock greater peace, fulfillment, and authenticity, both in your relationships and beyond.

WHAT ARE VALUES?

Values are the guiding principles that shape how you live your life. They are qualities of being, doing, and living that represent what we hold dear, what drives us, and what gives our lives meaning. For instance, honesty, respect, compassion, and loyalty are common values that people prioritize in their partnerships.

Values are things you do by choice that feel peaceful, satisfying, and personally fulfilling, not things you do out of obligation. Core values are not about how you think you "should" live, nor what you've been told by your parents, friends, teachers, or anyone else that you "should" value. They are the qualities of behavior you choose to prioritize because they resonate with your most authentic self.

Identifying Your Core Values

If you've completed the Relationship Vision and Values exercise in Chapter 2, you have already identified the values you hold personally and within the context of your relationship. If you have not yet completed this exercise, consider revisiting Chapter 2 and complete it now.

Review the list of values you made in Chapter 2 and begin to delve deeper into each one: How does it resonate with you on a personal level? Take a moment to reflect on each value and ask yourself:

- Does this value make me feel good about myself?
- Would living this value on a daily basis make me feel proud of who I am?
- Would I be comfortable and proud to share that this is one of my core values with those I love and respect?
- Would I stand by this value even if someone didn't share it?
- Can I see myself having a fulfilling life if I prioritize this value?
- Can I see myself having a meaningful relationship with a partner who shares this value?

If the answer to these questions is yes, that is indeed a core value of yours!

FEAR-BASED LIVING VS. VALUE-BASED LIVING

Knowing what your values are and living in alignment with them are two different things. Now that you have a good idea of your core values, it's time to check in with how often you're actually living them. Most people—especially those with relationship anxiety—find that while they often live in line with their values, they do slip into making decisions that aren't rooted in their values when their anxiety spikes. That's usually because in this fight-or-flight state, a doubt or fear has arisen that in the moment feels more powerful than their value. In this section, we'll explore what it looks like when you're making fear-based decisions versus value-based ones.

Fear-Based Living

Fear-based living is all about trying to avoid discomfort and uncertainty. It often leads to decisions driven by worry, insecurity, or external pressure instead of staying true to yourself and your values. In the context of relationships, fear-based living can manifest as:

- **Seesawing:** Fear of making the "wrong" decision might leave you living in a perpetual state of doubt and indecision. You may spend much of your time asking yourself things like: "Am I happy in this relationship? Is my partner good enough for me? Am I really in love with them? Is there someone better out there?" Thinking of staying in the relationship brings up anxiety, and thinking of leaving the relationship brings up an equal amount of anxiety. This places you in a continuous state of analysis, rumination, and flip-flopping between committing and leaving.

- **Avoiding vulnerability:** Fear of rejection or intimacy could lead you to avoid opening up to your partner or expressing your true feelings. It might also lead you to try to "think" your way through the relationship rather than allowing yourself to feel your feelings. You might try to convince yourself you are—or are not—really in love rather than allowing your true feelings to reveal themselves.
- **Partner-pleasing behavior:** Fear of conflict or disapproval could cause you to prioritize your partner's needs and opinions over your own, sacrificing your values and well-being in the process.
- **Comparison and self-doubt:** If you fear inadequacy or failure, you might start comparing your relationship to your friends' or family members' relationships. You might also regularly compare your current partner to previous partners to weigh the similarities and differences, attempting to ensure the "rightness" of your current partnership.
- **Seeking validation:** Fear of settling or fear of judgment can lead you to being overly reliant on others' approval of your relationship. You might even prioritize other people's opinions or approval of your partner over your own thoughts and feelings toward them.

These fear-based behaviors can erode trust, communication, and intimacy in relationships, ultimately hindering your ability to experience fulfillment and connection.

Value-Based Living

In contrast, value-based living means making choices that reflect your core values, even when fear or uncertainty arises. It's about prioritizing authenticity, integrity, hope, and personal growth in your decisions and actions. While you might not be able to find 100 percent certainty in your decision-making (no one can!), you can have confidence you're making choices that align with the qualities that are most important to you in life. In relationships, value-based living usually involves:

- **Commitment:** Assessing the quality of the relationship you have, then making a decision and sticking to it until you have clear, new evidence to the contrary.
- **Authentic communication:** Sharing your thoughts, feelings, and needs openly and honestly, even when it feels vulnerable.
- **Setting boundaries:** Respecting your own limits and boundaries and advocating for your needs and values within the relationship.
- **Embracing imperfection:** Accepting yourself and your partner as flawed yet inherently worthy individuals.
- **Self-validation:** Prioritizing your own approval of your partner over the approval of others and trusting that you know if your partner is a good fit for you better than anyone else can know.

When you embrace your values and make decisions that take them into account, you cultivate deeper connections, mutual respect, greater confidence, and a sense of purpose in your relationship.

Value-Based Living Leads to Greater Fulfillment in Life—and Relationships

As you strive to transition from fear-based living to value-based living, it's important to recognize there are no guarantees in life, regardless of the path you choose. Imagine yourself at 100 years old, reflecting on your life. What if you never took the leap to fully commit or confidently embrace relationship imperfections? Do you think a life spent anxiously seeking certainty about your partner would have been worth it? Or would finding joy within imperfection and intentionally settling with a partner who aligns with your values have offered more fulfillment?

Living a value-based life involves risks, but no more than living in fear. Letting your values guide your decisions means taking calculated risks toward your hopes and values rather than toward your fears and insecurities. Instead of seeking certainty about the future, consider asking yourself, "Does this decision feel right to me in this very moment? Is it aligned with my values to give this a solid chance?"

The essence of making value-based decisions lies in understanding that alignment with your values more often leads to a life you're proud of, despite the challenges. Fear-driven choices, on the other hand, often lead to deeper regret, shame, and resentment. While it doesn't guarantee a life free of pain or hardship, value-based living fosters a sense of pride, fulfillment, and internal alignment, regardless of the outcome. Even in the worst-case scenario, if your decisions are aligned with your values, it's easier to find solace and resilience amid disappointment and regret.

ACCEPTING SOME ANXIETY AS INEVITABLE

Swapping fear-based decision-making for value-based decision-making requires delving into a concept that may initially seem counterintuitive: accepting anxiety. Though this might seem backward initially, shifting your focus from trying to eliminate anxiety to embracing it proves effective!

This concept lies at the heart of Acceptance and Commitment Therapy (ACT), a therapeutic approach founded by Steven C. Hayes, PhD. Unlike some other therapeutic methods, ACT focuses on acceptance, mindfulness, and values-based action rather than challenging, stopping, or changing thoughts.

In overcoming relationship anxiety, it's key to acknowledge the inevitability of uncertainty. No matter how intentional your decisions or how vulnerable your communications, no relationship guarantees 100 percent certainty. This is where ACT can offer a powerful framework for shifting your perspective.

ACT encourages you to move from a stance of resistance to one of acceptance. Instead of struggling against anxious thoughts and feelings, it invites you to create space for them in your life without assigning them too much importance. This doesn't mean you have to like or agree with these anxious thoughts! It's about acknowledging their existence without judgment and moving forward in the direction of your goals, dreams, and values.

Through mindfulness practices and cognitive defusion techniques, ACT can help you detach from your unhelpful thoughts and beliefs. You can learn to observe your inner experience with openness and curiosity, then respond to your thoughts and feelings with judgment-free neutrality. This approach helps you move forward with meaningful, value-aligned action rather than compulsive behavior—even in the face of discomfort or uncertainty.

Cognitive Defusion, Defined

Cognitive defusion is a mindfulness technique aimed at creating distance from unhelpful thoughts. It's the process of observing thoughts as passing events in your mind rather than as facts, allowing you to reduce their impact and gain greater control over your responses. Cognitive defusion can take the form of noticing thoughts without judgment, thanking your mind for its creativity (even if it's making up false stories), singing your thoughts, or playfully mocking them.

Embracing acceptance as you manage anxiety offers many benefits that extend beyond tolerating uncomfortable thoughts and emotions. By cultivating an attitude of acceptance, you can experience profound shifts in your overall mental well-being and interpersonal relationships, including:

- **Reduced distress:** Acceptance offers you an opportunity to disengage from the struggle against unwanted thoughts and feelings, leading to less emotional distress. Rather than investing energy in resisting, suppressing, or analyzing anxious thoughts, acceptance offers a sense of calmness and confidence amid challenging circumstances. This reduction in distress can lead to improved emotional regulation and increased capacity to handle discomfort. It can also prevent your nervous system from becoming activated, allowing you to remain grounded and better able to make value-aligned decisions.

- **Increased psychological flexibility:** ACT emphasizes the development of psychological flexibility—in other words, the ability to adapt to the ever-changing demands of life. Through mindfulness practices and cognitive defusion techniques, you can learn to observe your thoughts and emotions with curiosity rather than getting entangled in them. This enhanced psychological flexibility enables you to navigate difficult situations with resilience and adaptability, leading to greater feelings of control and empowerment.

- **More happiness in your relationship:** Practicing acceptance can significantly improve your relationship by increasing empathy, understanding, and connection with your partner. When you accept your own thoughts and emotions without judgment, you're better equipped to extend that same level of acceptance to your partner. This creates an atmosphere of emotional safety and vulnerability in the relationship. Additionally, embracing acceptance reduces the tendency to engage in controlling or avoidant behaviors, leading to healthier patterns of interaction and increased intimacy.

- **Confidence building:** Acceptance not only helps in navigating challenging thoughts and feelings—it also builds confidence. Being able to confront and manage situations that once caused distress enhances feelings of pride and self-assurance. Recognizing that your anxiety doesn't have to call the shots in your life leads to greater feelings of happiness and a sense of freedom.

Acceptance in Action

So, how do values and acceptance translate into action? Picture having the thought that your family might not think your partner is "good enough" for you. This thought makes you feel uncomfortable, which could lead to potential compulsive reactions, such as seeking reassurance from your family, mentally reviewing past interactions for signs of disapproval, or even considering canceling plans to avoid potential judgment. All these responses operate under the assumption your initial thought is significant. Engaging in rumination, mental review, or avoidance would signal to your brain that this thought deserves your active attention.

Acceptance and value-aligned action, on the other hand, would involve a thought process like this: "What if my family doesn't think my partner is good enough for me? That's an interesting thought. If that were true, I would be disappointed because I value my family's opinion. However, I trust myself and believe that my partner and I are good for each other. While I'd love everyone to think highly of my partner, I understand I am not responsible for other people's thoughts or feelings, only my own. Because I value time with both my family and my partner, I'm going to the event and will be as present as possible."

Keep in mind that the goal here is to practice accepting your thoughts and feelings with neutrality. They're not good; they're not bad….They just *are*. You are in control of how you respond, regardless of what your thoughts are telling you. Practicing acceptance in this way will slowly teach your brain that these intrusive thoughts are not meaningful or dangerous. With continued practice, you will learn that it is possible to have intrusive, confusing, or uncomfortable thoughts and not have to respond at all. Remember that the journey toward anxiety recovery is not about dissecting your thoughts but about choosing which thoughts are worthy of your time and energy.

The example about whether your family likes your partner highlights the difference between fear-based living and value-based living. Fear-based living is attempting to avoid the discomfort or uncertainty around your family potentially not liking your partner. Value-based living is accepting that as a possibility without engaging with the thought. It is choosing to move forward with spending time with your family and your partner despite the uncertainty because you understand that you value quality time with the ones you love more than you value having certainty.

TRY USING NON-ENGAGEMENT RESPONSES TO REFOCUS ON YOUR VALUES

Non-engagement responses (NERs), developed by psychologist Lisa Levine, PsyD, are statements that purposefully call out discomfort or uncertainty rather than attempting to deny their existence. These responses can support you in actively disengaging from your anxious thoughts and doubts.

Examples of NERs

When you use NERs, you're essentially telling your brain, "I hear you. Thank you for your input, but I'm choosing to prioritize actions that are aligned with my values instead of fear-based thinking." You can think of the practice of NERs as affirming your thoughts where you can while maintaining your autonomy over your actions. For example, if your brain says, "I'm feeling anxious that I don't know for sure if my partner is 'The One,'" you could respond with "You're right, I don't know for sure if they are the one, and not knowing for sure is difficult for me to sit with." You've affirmed your feelings of anxiety, uncertainty, and discomfort without overanalyzing or dissecting the thoughts and feelings any further.

Here are a couple of other examples of possible NERs:

- **The thought that you don't love your partner:** On the way to dinner, you have the thought: "What if I'm leading my partner on and I don't really love them?"
  - **Fear-based reaction:** Confessing to your partner you're not sure you really love them, choosing not to go to dinner, or

spending the entire dinner checking your feelings toward your partner.

- **Value-based NER:** Recognizing this as a fear-based thought, you pause and acknowledge it without allowing it to dictate your actions. You affirm to yourself, "There I go again, having the thought I might not love my partner," but instead of canceling plans or obsessing over your feelings, you choose to focus back on the present moment and the enjoyment of spending time with your partner. You remind yourself that while it feels uncomfortable not knowing for sure, love is a complex emotion that can fluctuate, and it's okay to experience doubts from time to time. By choosing to prioritize the connection and companionship you share with your partner, you reaffirm your commitment to nurturing the relationship, even amid anxiety and uncertainty.

- **Social gathering:** After receiving an invitation to a party, you think, "What if there are people I (or my partner) find attractive at the party?"

  - **Fear-based reaction:** Declining the invitation to avoid the possibility of being around people you (or your partner) find attractive.

  - **Value-based NER:** Instead of succumbing to the fear of potential temptation or jealousy, you choose to focus on the value of social connection and shared experiences. You affirm to yourself that it's possible there will be people there that you (or your partner) find attractive and that feelings of attraction are natural and don't threaten the strength of your relationship. By attending the party with your partner, you affirm your trust in each other and your commitment to mutual respect and honesty. Rather than avoiding situations that trigger insecurity, you choose to embrace opportunities for fun, connection, and growth because these are important to you in your life and relationships.

NERs Give You Power over Fear-Based Thoughts

It's important to note that NERs are not an attempt to stop your anxious thoughts entirely but rather to shift your attention *away* from responding to the thoughts and *toward* engaging with something more value-aligned instead. They help you block your compulsive response, not block your anxious thoughts. Using NERs teaches the anxious part of your brain that *you* are in charge of where you put your time and mental energy and that you're choosing to focus on value-aligned thoughts and activities rather than fear-based ones.

Utilizing these statements is a way of demonstrating to yourself that the content of your thoughts truly isn't significant and that your thoughts and subsequent anxiety will eventually pass on their own, even if you don't try to force them away. In the long run, this process will help you build confidence and give the content of your thoughts less importance.

NERs are closely related to the concept of practicing acceptance, which we discussed earlier in this chapter. NERs help you accept the presence of the thought, not the accuracy or inaccuracy of what it's telling you. Just because something *could* happen or *could* be true doesn't mean you're accepting it *will* happen or *is* true. You're simply entertaining the idea that while it's a possibility, it's not a possibility you're going to spend more of your precious time on in this moment.

It's also essential to understand that incorporating NERs into your life requires patience, persistence, and self-compassion. When you've been engaging with your anxious or intrusive thoughts for years, practicing non-engagement will take some practice. Like any other skill, the time and effort you put into practicing non-engagement will be worth it when you are better able to manage relationship anxiety long term.

> Case Study: Mid-Spiral Turnaround

Gwen found herself driving home from a date with her partner of one year feeling a sense of disappointment and doubt. As she replayed the evening's events in her mind, she couldn't shake the nagging thought: I didn't have fun tonight. Maybe we're not really connected, and our life together will be boring.

In the past, Gwen would have spiraled into a cycle of overanalysis and self-doubt. She would have spent hours reviewing previous dates, questioning the connection between her and her partner, and worrying about the future of their relationship. However, Gwen had been actively practicing non-engagement responses when her anxiety kicked in, and she was determined not to let fear dictate her actions.

Catching herself mid-spiral, she took a deep breath and reminded herself of her commitment to value-based living. Instead of allowing the disappointment to overshadow the entire relationship with her partner, she chose to acknowledge the disappointment without judgment. She affirmed to herself that perhaps the evening hadn't met her expectations, but that didn't diminish the connection she shared with her partner.

Rather than dwelling on perceived shortcomings or past experiences, Gwen chose to focus on the present moment. She engaged in conversation with her partner, cherishing the opportunity to share stories and laughter together, even if their evening was less than ideal. She reminded herself that every relationship has its ups and downs, and one less-than-perfect date didn't define the totality of their connection.

UNDERSTAND HOW PREFERENCES ARE DIFFERENT THAN VALUES

An important aspect of managing relationship anxiety lies in figuring out the difference between values and preferences. While both factors influence your interactions and decisions, understanding how they're distinct can shape how you navigate decision-making in relationships.

- **Values** are your fundamental beliefs, guiding principles, and nonnegotiables that are foundational to your sense of self and how you engage with the world. These are qualities such as integrity, thoughtfulness, and kindness that resonate deeply with your core being and reflect what you hold sacred in your relationships.
- **Preferences** encompass the myriad of desires, likings, and quirks that enhance your interactions but aren't necessarily deal-breakers or integral to your identity. These can range from matters like food preferences or leisure activities to more significant considerations, such as lifestyle choices or aesthetic preferences. Preferences are inherently subjective and could be influenced by personal experiences, family traditions, and individual personalities.

When faced with dilemmas or uncertainties, leaning into your values rather than fixating on preferences can offer clarity and direction. For example, let's imagine your partner prefers spontaneous outings while you prefer more well-planned adventures. While these preferences could initially seem incompatible, they don't have to be sources of conflict or tension if they don't compromise your shared values, say, values of mutual respect, connection, and adventure. Maybe you can find a balance where sometimes the adventures are planned in advance and other times they're more spontaneous. While you might not be fulfilling the preferences of both of you each time, you are still fulfilling your shared values of adventure, connection, and respect.

It's important to recognize that embracing your values over your preferences is not about suppressing your desires or denying your authenticity. Instead, it's an empowering choice to prioritize what truly matters to you in the long run: building a relationship founded on trust, generosity, and shared values. This in turn can help you both find common ground and learn to explore preferential differences with kindness and understanding.

BE OPEN TO VALUES THAT SHIFT

While many of your core values remain steadfast across different stages and circumstances throughout your life, some might change. Just as you grow and evolve as individuals, so too can some of your values undergo shifts in response to changing circumstances, experiences, and priorities.

- **Fixed values** tend to be more unwavering, and might include values such as honesty, integrity, compassion, authenticity, and loyalty. If these are important to you now, they'll probably always be important to you, regardless of which stage of life you're in.
- **Dynamic values** are more fluid, adaptable, and responsive to the shifts in your life. They are influenced by external factors such as relationships, career transitions, parenthood, or personal growth journeys. Let's say you currently prioritize independence and adventure. Several years down the road, the arrival of children could prompt a shift in focus toward nurturing, stability, and interdependence. Similarly, while you might value having a large home or luxurious car, the loss of a job or change in financial status could create a shift in what you value materialistically.

It's freeing to grant yourself permission to embrace the evolving nature of your values without judgment. As you progress through life, you might find that certain values resonate more deeply with your current circumstances, while others recede into the background or get redefined. These shifts are not necessarily signs of inconsistency or moral ambiguity but rather a testament to your capacity for growth, adaptation, and self-discovery.

Take the time to periodically revisit, reassess, and/or redefine your values, examining how they align with your current aspirations, relationships, and life circumstances. Reflect on the experiences that have shaped your values, acknowledging any lessons learned or wisdom gained along the way. Remain open to changing your mind and adjusting your values when new perspectives and life experiences warrant it.

Exercise:
Thought and Behavior Reevaluation

Revisit what you came up with for the Thought and Behavior Log exercise from Chapter 3. Hopefully you have a clear list of the thoughts and/or behaviors that are causing you distress and keeping you stuck. In this exercise, we're going to practice incorporating acceptance and non-engagement responses into your current list.

Go through your list, and under each thought/behavior, write down how you could approach it differently in the future practicing acceptance rather than compulsive behavior. You can use the following example as a guide.

- **Thought:** What if my partner and I are not compatible enough?
- **Compulsive behavior:** Confessing to your partner you aren't sure if you like and want enough of the same things they do, checking for areas of compatibility or lack thereof, and/or asking your friends and family how they know they're compatible with their partners.
- **Acceptance and Non-Engagement Response:** "There I go again, having the thought I might not be compatible enough with my partner. I get so uncomfortable when that thought arises. Anyway, I'd better get going or I'll be late for work."

Practice, practice, practice! Repatterning the brain can take time. Do your best to be compassionate with yourself along the way. Progress, no matter how small, adds up over time!

Note: While you can benefit from practicing acceptance on your own, if you're feeling stuck or like you could use additional support, consider working with a professional trained in ACT for individualized guidance. You can also consider reading *The Happiness Trap: How to Stop Struggling and Start Living* by Russ Harris or visiting Steven C. Hayes, PhD's website, both included on the Resource List at the back of this book, for additional information on ACT.

Key Takeaways

- Making value-based rather than fear-based decisions will make you feel more content in your relationship and lead to feelings of greater confidence, pride, and resilience, regardless of the outcome.
- Practice acceptance. Rather than resisting or suppressing anxious thoughts, learn to observe them without judgment, allowing them to come and go while prioritizing actions aligned with your values.
- Responding to anxious thoughts with NERs can redirect your focus toward value-aligned actions and allow you to take your power back from the grip of anxiety, insecurity, and uncertainty.

CHAPTER 9

NAVIGATING COMPARISONS, OPINIONS, AND SOCIAL MEDIA

Think of a time when you scrolled through your social media feed, stopping to admire the seemingly perfect relationships in each carefully curated post. Did you find yourself comparing your own love life to those snapshots of happiness? If so, you're in good company—so many people do that!

Our relationships are deeply intertwined with the world around us. From advice from family and friends to the relentless scrutiny of social media, there are so many outside factors that affect your relationship. Amid the constant barrage of opinions, judgments, and comparisons, it's easy to lose sight of your own truth. Allowing external factors to influence how you feel about your relationship not only robs you of your joy but also chips away at your self-trust, gratitude, peace, and more.

In the upcoming chapter, we'll examine the many types of external influences that impact your relationship, from the well-meaning advice of loved ones, to the expectations set through social media, to the pressures of societal norms. You will then learn practical strategies for discerning between helpful feedback and unnecessary noise. If you are able to practice internal validation instead of external validation, you will find yourself living by your values and more connected to your partner.

WHY DO WE COMPARE OURSELVES TO OTHERS IN THE FIRST PLACE?

Comparison is a natural part of the human experience. We all size up ourselves against others in various aspects of our lives. At its core, comparison can actually serve as a valuable tool for survival and growth, allowing us to learn from others and adapt as needed. However, when comparison becomes excessive or when we idealize others' relationships, it can become detrimental.

If you're dealing with relationship anxiety, the tendency to compare yourself to others can be all-consuming. You might constantly feel doubt and uncertainty and look to others' lives in search of answers about the state of your own relationship. Whether it's scrolling through social media feeds and seeing seemingly effortless loving relationships or comparing relationship milestones with friends and family, the urge to measure up usually only leads to feelings of inadequacy and shame.

But the thing is, relationships aren't a competition. Love and happiness do not come with a scorecard. Comparing your own worst moments to someone else's best only distorts reality and leaves you feeling disheartened and more confused about your own relationship. It's like giving up your favorite hobby to pursue something you're not interested in just because everyone else seems to enjoy it. In doing so, you forget you were already content with your own interests before you tried to be more like others. As you search for clarity around your relationship, try not to let other people's apparent happiness overshadow your own contentment.

Common Areas of Comparison

While comparison can happen anywhere and everywhere, some of the more common areas of comparison in relationships include:

- **Emotional connection:** Comparing the depth of emotional intimacy or connection in your relationship to that of others, such as expression of emotions, levels of thoughtfulness, or emotional support.

- **Happiness levels:** Comparing your own relationship happiness to the perceived happiness of others, such has how often you're laughing together or sharing smile-filled photos.
- **Sex lives:** Comparing the frequency or quality of your sex life with that of others.
- **Physical attractiveness:** Comparing your own appearance or attractiveness to that of others, including your partner's exes (or vice versa).
- **Milestones/personal achievements:** Comparing relationship milestones, like a marriage proposal, or personal achievements to those of friends or peers.
- **Public displays of affection (PDAs):** Comparing how your partner displays affection publicly—whether in person or on social media—to how others do.
- **Family/friend relationships:** Comparing others' relationships with their partners' family and friends to your own or comparing how your family/friends treat your partner compared to how they treat other people's partners.
- **Status and stability:** Comparing your partner's education, career, car, home, or financial status to others. This category also includes comparing how household and financial responsibilities are shared.
- **Parenting styles:** Comparing your approach to parenting with others', including philosophies, disciplinary methods, approach to schooling, or dynamics within the relationship.
- **Leisure activities:** Comparing the leisure activities or hobbies you and your partner enjoy in your relationship to those of others, including how and where you spend your free time and the level of excitement or adventure.
- **Feelings of love:** Comparing your feelings of love with your partner to those you perceive in others' relationships.

Whether you see yourself reflected in these examples or you catch yourself comparing other aspects of your relationship, remember that comparison isn't necessarily a reflection of reality. It often presents a skewed perspective that ignores the uniqueness of your relationship.

Happiness Is Not a Competition

Happiness is not a zero-sum game. Someone else being happy and fulfilled in their relationship does not mean you cannot be happy and fulfilled in your own relationship. What works for someone else may not work for you, and that's okay. Contentment in relationships comes from understanding your own needs, values, and desires—not from trying to keep up with someone else's relationship.

Another important thing to know: Happy couples aren't preoccupied with whether others are happier. They're too busy being content and continuing to prioritize their own happiness. You can do the same! Rather than letting comparison bring you down, view it as a way to highlight things you'd like more of in your own life. Identify what it is that you admire in others and take practical steps toward cultivating those qualities in your own relationship (more on that next).

Each relationship is unique, and there's no one-size-fits-all approach to happiness. Celebrate your individuality, and when you're tempted to compare, do your best to prioritize what matters most to *you* and *your* partner. By focusing on your own relationship, you'll find greater satisfaction and fulfillment than by comparing yourself to others.

Use Comparison to Inspire Authentic Change

Instead of allowing comparison to breed insecurity, do your best to use it as a catalyst for positive change. You can compare more mindfully by checking in with yourself with questions such as:

- What is it about this person/couple that I admire?
- What qualities or experiences does this person/couple have that I am envious of?
- Do I have, or have I ever had, something similar in my own partnership?
- How can I work toward incorporating these qualities/behaviors into my own life and relationship?

For example, if you admire a couple's ability to have fun together, ask yourself when you last experienced having fun with your partner. Your answer could serve as a reminder that you already have similar aspects in your own relationship. If you can't think of the last time you've done something fun with your partner—and having fun together is a core value of yours—use this realization as an opportunity to communicate with your partner. Explore ways to incorporate more fun and enjoyment into your lives together. Dwelling in someone else's happiness isn't going to make you happier, but taking value-aligned action in your own life just might.

RELATIONSHIP ANXIETY AND SOCIAL MEDIA

Social media can often feel like a double-edged sword, especially when it comes to relationships. It's a place where we connect, share, and receive validation, but it's also a breeding ground for comparison and self-doubt. It's essential to recognize that what you see on social media is not the full story. While you're scrolling through picture-perfect moments and envy-inducing updates, you must remember that these snapshots rarely reflect the nuance and complexities of real life.

Have you ever seen those short clips with captions like "Find yourself a partner who looks at you the way so-and-so looks at their partner"? While initially cute and harmless, they can quickly lead to a spiral of self-doubt. Questions such as "Why doesn't my partner look at me that way?" or "Why don't they engage in cute activities or social trends with me?" may start to surface. However, it's important to understand that these are curated *moments*, not a full representation of a relationship. These clips might even be scripted, rehearsed, or forced, so they're not even real to begin with. Regardless of the stories your brain comes up with, you truly do not know the intricacies of others' experiences beyond what is presented.

How Does Social Media Affect Your Thinking?

Think for a moment about how social media impacts your own relationship:

- How often have you seen someone post a cute couple photo with a heartfelt, sentimental caption about finally finding their soulmate…only to see that person completely deleted from their social media feed (and their life) a few months later?
- How often has a friend vented to you about their vacation, only to post about the vacation on social media with extravagant photos and a caption that reads "Take me back"?
- How many times have you come across holiday snapshots filled with smiles despite knowing that the family behind the screen is struggling with their own challenges?
- How many times have *you* shared a smiley photo while on the inside you've been filled with doubt and anxiety?

The truth is, much of the time, social media is an edited highlight reel, not an accurate depiction of reality. Of course, it doesn't mean everything you're seeing is fake, but it does mean even the posts that are authentic merely offer glimpses into moments of authenticity, not the entirety of a relationship.

Even Negative Posts Can Cause Anxiety

Comparison can even strike among those who are sharing their hardships or imperfections. Keep in mind that even sharing challenges is often done in a polished and well-worded manner, far removed from the raw and unfiltered truth. If you're not cognizant of this fact, the curated authenticity can leave you feeling even more isolated in your struggles, as you compare your messy reality to others' carefully crafted narratives. Here's an example:

Polished post: "With love and appreciation for one another, we've decided to part ways. Our priority remains our children, and we are dedicated to raising them together as friends and partners in parenting. #consciousuncoupling #coparentinggoals"

Real post: "This divorce has been incredibly tough. We're trying to co-parent, but the constant arguments make it almost impossible. The kids are caught in the middle, and it breaks my heart. I'm struggling to navigate the anger and hurt while trying to be a good parent."

Use Social Media Mindfully

How can you navigate this minefield of comparison and self-doubt and take back your power? It's first essential to use social media as mindfully and intentionally as possible. As you scroll, ask yourself:

- Does this content inspire, motivate, and encourage me, or does it have the opposite effect?
- Do I feel better or worse about myself and my relationship after viewing it?
- Is this entertaining me or triggering me?
- Is this a good use of my time, or could it be been better spent elsewhere?

Remember that comparison is natural, but it's also a slippery slope. Rather than getting lost in someone else's highlight reel, feeling worse and worse about yourself in the process, try to find moments of relatability and common ground. Remind yourself that you're not alone in your struggles and that many others are grappling with similar feelings of inadequacy and self-doubt, no matter what their social media feed presents.

> Case Study: Envious of a Facade

Sasha found herself in a constant state of comparison as she scrolled through her social media feeds. Each picture-perfect post seemed to showcase the epitome of happiness and love, leaving her feeling inadequate in her own relationship. She couldn't help but compare her partner to those she saw online.

One day, Sasha stumbled on a particularly envy-inducing post from an acquaintance, Cora. Cora's feed was filled with romantic getaways, candlelit dinners, and heartfelt declarations of love. Sasha couldn't shake the feeling of inadequacy as she compared Cora's seemingly perfect relationship to her own. While she knew she loved her partner, she couldn't stop herself from wondering if she was settling for less than the best with them. Was there someone else she could have an even deeper connection and more romantic relationship with?

However, Sasha's perspective shifted dramatically when she ran into Cora at a mutual friend's party. Expecting to see the embodiment of relationship bliss, she was surprised to find Cora in tears, confiding in a friend about her partner's repeated infidelity.

This encounter served as a wake-up call. Sasha realized that what she saw on social media was merely a curated facade, masking the challenges in Cora's true relationship. Her envy of Cora's relationship was replaced with feelings of sadness for Cora and gratitude for the relationship she had with her partner.

THE PROBLEM WITH SEEKING FEEDBACK FROM LOVED ONES

Of course, loved ones can also impact your relationship in many ways. While it's natural to seek validation and approval from your family and friends regarding your relationship, if you're struggling with relationship anxiety, you are more likely to take it to the extreme. Valuing the opinions of your loved ones is understandable, but you shouldn't place their thoughts and judgments above your own.

Similar to navigating social media and being mindful of comparison, it's equally important to consider how you consume feedback and opinions from those in your inner circle. One key aspect of this is being careful who you share details of your relationship with and whose advice you seek.

Especially during moments of doubt and uncertainty, the temptation to vent to someone—*anyone*—can be strong. Yet even in this state of anxiety, you should really consider who you talk to. Not all advice is created equal, and not everyone in your inner circle will provide sound guidance despite their good intentions.

Are They a Good Match for Your Values?

Before sharing, ask yourself the following:

- Do you share similar values and a comparable relationship vision?
- When this person has offered advice in the past, did it tend to be helpful or harmful?
- Do you believe they understand you deeply enough to provide accurate feedback and advice?
- Do you truly value and respect who they are as human beings and the way they live their life?

If the answer to these questions isn't a resounding yes, it may not be worth your time and energy to divulge details of your relationship.

Everyone Has Their Own Baggage

Most people filter their opinions through their own lens, which is shaped by their own life experiences. For example, your aunt might offer advice based on her own miserable marriage, your mom might draw parallels to your dad's actions despite your relationship being completely different, your brother might share what he thinks is best based on his very different life goals, and your friend who's been burned by an ex might advise against trusting anyone.

The bottom line is that others' experiences might not align with your situation. Ultimately, no one knows you better than you know yourself, and sometimes the more advice you seek, the more confused you become. With each person's feedback and opinion, your own truth gets diluted more and more, and the pressure to please others might sway you away from trusting yourself altogether. It's okay to care about what other people think and want, but it's just as important to check in with yourself to ensure you're not caring what *they* think of your relationship more than what *you* think of your relationship.

Be Careful When Venting

If and when you do choose to share or ask the opinion of others, keep in mind that while venting can sometimes be cathartic, you might regret it later. Frequent airing of doubts and grievances can not only strain your relationship but also lead to unintended consequences, such as a misrepresentation of your partnership or unsolicited and unhelpful advice. Balanced sharing is key. Here are some guidelines for venting more mindfully:

- Consider setting healthy boundaries, such as limiting venting sessions.
- Select confidants who respect your relationship's privacy.
- Remember that once you share, you can't take it back.

It's reasonable to need to get things off your chest from time to time, but sharing too much too frequently can lead to feelings of awkwardness in future interactions, followed by overexplaining to course correct. That's why it's important to do your best to maintain a balance between seeking support and protecting the privacy and sanctity of your relationship.

Don't Dodge Your Own Responsibility

Seeking advice from others can sometimes be your anxiety attempting to shift responsibility away from you and onto someone else. By relying on someone else's judgment, you might feel a sense of relief from the burden of decision-making. While it could provide temporary relief to have someone else to "blame" if things go awry, true growth and fulfillment come from taking ownership of your choices.

Try to find pride and responsibility in making decisions, particularly those concerning your own life. When it comes to seeking advice about your relationship, it's crucial to strike a balance between external input, value alignment, and trust in your own judgment and intuition.

No One's Opinion Is More Valid Than Yours

Ultimately, remember that you do not need to convince others why you are in your relationship. You don't need to prove to others that your partner is great (or not) and you don't need to explain why you're choosing to stay with (or leave) them. You don't need to explain your decisions, period. As uncomfortable as this may be to accept, it's okay for people to not understand, to misunderstand, or to misjudge your relationship. Frankly, no one's life will be more deeply affected by the partner you choose than your own, and therefore, no one will care about who you choose as a partner more than you do. This isn't to say no one cares about you or your happiness; it's just that everyone is so caught up living their own life and focused on themselves to care more than you do about the partner you choose.

TRUST YOUR INNER VOICE

Your ability to minimize the effect of external voices on your relationship is stronger if you are able to trust your own instincts. You may be thinking, "But I don't know what my intuition is telling me!"

Have you ever put on an outfit you're excited about only to have someone criticize it, immediately replacing your initial excitement with doubt and insecurity? There is a similar effect when you seek too many outside opinions regarding your relationship. While external advice can certainly be helpful, at times it may introduce unnecessary hurt and confusion when you were already content without it.

So how do you know whether you're anxiously venting and/or relying too heavily on someone else's input on your relationships when you could instead be relying on yourself? One helpful exercise is to pause before running a question by someone and ask yourself, "What do I hope this person will say?" For instance, if you ask someone's opinion about your partner and feel disappointed when they express negativity, it may indicate that you were hoping for a stamp of approval because you genuinely love them and are content with your partnership. Perhaps what you were looking for was someone's approval of your decision, not their opinion on your decision.

Another way to safeguard against unnecessary opinions of others is to ask yourself if you genuinely don't know the answer or if you do already know the answer and are looking for reassurance. Sometimes, deep down, we already know the answer, but we turn to others in hopes of validation. Reflect on whether this is a situation where someone else might genuinely have better insight than you, or you know the answer yourself. For example, a question about whether they think you have sex often enough, travel together enough, or spend enough money on one another is not something someone else would know the answer to better than you. Everyone has different needs, capabilities, and resources, and no one can answer such questions better than you can answer them yourself.

Whenever possible, prioritize going inward to answer and validate yourself. Ultimately, the opinions of your friends and family, while important, pale in comparison to your own. Your happiness and fulfillment in your relationship should be guided by your own needs, values, feelings, and relationship goals and vision.

Remember, if you're miserable in a relationship your family loves, you're still miserable. Conversely, if you're content in a relationship your family doesn't love, you're still content. Be mindful of whether you're living for the approval of others or for your own happiness. Ask yourself honestly, "How will my life genuinely be better if everyone likes my partner?" The most important thing is that *you* feel good about your partner, and that's why it's important to trust in your own judgment and prioritize your own well-being above external validation.

PRACTICE RELATIONSHIP SELF-CONFIDENCE

Confidence can be a game changer when it comes to how your relationship is perceived by others, especially your family and friends. Think about the relationships you admire most—chances are, the partners speak highly of each other, exude confidence, and radiate positivity. When you present your partner with confidence, it sends a powerful message to those around you.

Now take a moment to consider how you present your partner to others. Your friends obviously want to see you happy, so if you consistently appear stressed or anxious around your partner, they may jump to conclusions about the relationship. If you constantly micromanage interactions with your partner out of anxiety, others may pick up on it, potentially casting a negative light on your relationship. Especially if they're not familiar with relationship anxiety, they might not realize that your behavior stems from relationship anxiety rather than genuine relationship issues.

No Relationship Is Perfect
Remember, the relationships you admire still probably have periods of boredom, conflict, and dissatisfaction—it's just more likely they're choosing not to showcase those periods every time you're with them.

On the other hand, if you speak confidently and lovingly about your partner and take time to speak about the things you love about them—in addition to the areas of concern—your friends are more likely to see the positive aspects of your relationship. What you choose to focus on tends to grow, not only for yourself but also for others.

The next time you're around family or friends, try sharing the things you genuinely like and admire about your partner and notice how it changes the dynamic. It's not about pretending or being inauthentic; instead, it's about intentionally choosing to hold your head high, be proud of yourself and your partner, and focus on the positive aspects of your relationship more regularly when you're around others.

Exercise:
Reflect Before Seeking Advice

Taking the time to pause and reflect can help you make a more conscious and informed decision about whether you really need to ask for advice and opinions regarding your relationship. Next time, before talking to someone else about your relationship, ask yourself about your own motivations and expectations using these questions:

- **What am I hoping this person says right now?** Consider whether you're seeking validation, reassurance, or a specific answer to confirm your own beliefs or desires.
- **What advice am I hoping to hear?** Reflect on whether you're looking for guidance that aligns with what you want to hear, or you're genuinely seeking objective advice.
- **Do I really need to get their opinion, or do I already know (but maybe not like) the answer?** Consider whether you're seeking external validation to avoid facing a truth you may already be aware of but find difficult to accept.
- **Is their answer more likely to give me clarity or make me feel more confused?** Evaluate whether seeking advice from this person

is likely to provide genuine insight and understanding or might add to your uncertainty and confusion.

- **Am I seeking permission to stay in or end this relationship?** If you could know with certainty that everything would be okay, regardless of what decision you make around your relationship, what would you do?

Answering these questions encourages self-awareness and mindfulness in your interactions with others. This process can empower you to trust your own judgment and intuition, whether you choose to move forward with running the scenario by someone else or not.

Key Takeaways

- While comparison is a natural human tendency, excessive comparison leads to feelings of insecurity and dissatisfaction. The stories you create about other relationships may or may not be true, and the energy you spend evaluating others' relationships would be better spent improving your own.
- Social media often presents a curated version of reality, which can trigger feelings of inadequacy and doubt. Remember that what you see on social media may not accurately reflect the reality, or totality, of others' relationships. Practice mindfulness when engaging with social media content.
- While seeking feedback from loved ones can be valuable, it's essential to trust your own judgment and desires above all else. Reflect on your own needs and values, prioritize your opinion of your partner above others' opinions, and be mindful of who you share with and why you're sharing if/when you choose to do so.

CHAPTER 10

COMMUNICATING AND CO-REGULATING WITH YOUR PARTNER

Imagine carrying a heavy backpack on a long hike, the weight pressing down on your shoulders with each step. At first, it may seem manageable, but as the miles stretch on, the pain becomes less and less bearable. There is someone by your side willing to lighten the load, but you don't want to burden them, so you smile and trek on. You hide the pain you're in until it becomes totally unbearable and you stop altogether. Now the hike is at a standstill because you were trying to bear it all for too long. Now, imagine if you shared the weight with the person beside you before it got unbearable. Not only would you have actually finished the hike, but you'd have had a better time along the way.

Relationship anxiety can feel like that heavy backpack. Just as sharing the backpack can make a hike more manageable, opening up to your partner about your anxiety can lighten the emotional burden you carry. This chapter will explore the power of sharing your struggles with your partner, including how vulnerable conversations can lead to deeper connection. It will also discuss how to navigate the delicate balance of sharing your anxiety without *over*sharing and help you discern which information is helpful to share and which is better kept private. Lastly, this chapter will cover the importance of bonding and healing together, helping you see how shared experiences and rituals can strengthen your connection and provide a sense of support in times of uncertainty.

START THE CONVERSATION

Opening up about relationship anxiety may feel scary, especially since you might be uncertain about how your partner will respond and might worry about them judging you. Will they understand? Will their feelings be hurt? Will they think differently of you? These are valid concerns, but ultimately you can't control their response, only your own. While you always have the power to decide if, when, and what you choose to share regarding your anxiety, choosing to do so can be a crucial step toward increasing understanding and building a stronger, more resilient bond with your partner.

While anxiety may make you feel otherwise, it's important to recognize that experiencing relationship anxiety doesn't mean you're "broken" or less deserving of love. You're choosing to share with your partner because you care about and trust them—and remember that your feelings are just as important as theirs!

When to Bring It Up

Before you begin to share details of your anxiety, it's helpful to consider your mental state. If you're feeling insecure, triggered, or self-critical, it may not be the best time to bring up the topic. While your mindset alone won't determine the success of the conversation, it can influence its direction. You have a higher probability of having a compassionate, productive exchange if you're feeling motivated and at least somewhat confident than if you're feeling shameful or triggered. With this in mind, something to consider asking yourself before you initiate the conversation with your partner is why you want to share this with them right now.

Answering this question can help you figure out what's motivating your desire to share. Are you telling your partner about your doubts because you're feeling panicked and you need to let it out? Are you feeling guilty and want to share so you don't feel like you're lying? Are you feeling insecure and you're sharing in hopes of receiving reassurance?

If you notice you're being motivated by a desire to get reassurance or alleviate guilt, it may be better to table the conversation until you're feeling more grounded and secure. However, if you genuinely desire to be vulnerable to deepen your emotional connection, it may be the right time to share.

Timing is especially important when discussing vulnerable topics or matters that require your partner's undivided energy and attention. Asking your partner if it's a good time to chat shows consideration of their physical and emotional bandwidth and sets the stage for a more focused and receptive dialogue. Do your best to avoid moments such as when you're rushing out the door, meeting friends for dinner, or winding down after a hectic day, as these may not provide an ideal environment for a meaningful discussion.

How to Broach the Topic

Here are a couple examples of conversation openers:

- I've figured some things out lately, and I'd love to share them with you. Is now a good time to talk?
- I've been learning about something I've been wanting to discuss with you. When would be a good time for us to have a conversation?

If your partner seems caught off guard and asks what you want to talk about, you can provide a quick, honest explanation and mention that it's about anxiety, mental health, or self-trust. Keep in mind that regularly checking in with your partner before conversations about timing can help normalize these discussions and alleviate anticipatory anxiety going forward.

No Time Is Perfect

It's important to note there's never a perfect time to have these conversations; waiting for the stars to align will only lead to unnecessary delay. If your partner indicates that now isn't the right time, try not to be discouraged. View this as your partner setting a healthy boundary, and ask them when would be a better time to connect.

BE VULNERABLE

Whether it's the first time you're bringing up the topic of relationship anxiety, or you're revisiting the topic again, letting your partner know that discussing this topic is challenging for you opens the door to a gentler, more receptive interaction. Vulnerability can be contagious—when you lower your defenses, you invite your partner to listen actively and respond with empathy instead of defensiveness. This sets the stage for a supportive dialogue where both of you engage with patience, compassion, and a genuine desire to understand each other.

Here are some examples of how you could express your vulnerability:

- I'm feeling a bit nervous to bring this up, but our relationship is important to me, so I want to share my thoughts with you.
- I appreciate your willingness to listen. This topic is challenging for me to talk about, so I may stumble over my words, but I'll do my best.
- Sharing this is hard, but I believe it can bring us closer as a couple, so I'll try to articulate my feelings as best as I can.
- Although we've discussed this before—and you've been so supportive—it's still difficult for me to bring it up again.

If nerves start to overwhelm you, remind yourself that approaching your partner with vulnerability is an act of courage likely to bring you two closer together. Sharing about your anxiety signals trust, respect, and a commitment to strengthening your relationship. Inviting your partner into this aspect of your life is a gift to them, just as it's a gift to you when they choose to share intimate details with you. While it might seem easier to avoid vulnerability, your willingness to risk discomfort is a testament to your resilience and determination to create a secure, honest partnership.

Vulnerability vs. Manipulation

While vulnerability is essential for deepening emotional intimacy in a relationship, you should only share what feels true and authentic. The goal is to utilize vulnerability as a means to connect, not manipulate. Authentic vulnerability fosters trust, empathy, and connection, whereas manipulative vulnerability can erode trust and create distance in the relationship.

Authentic vulnerability is the process of opening up and expressing your true feelings, needs, and experiences in a genuine, transparent manner, even when it's challenging or uncomfortable. You're essentially inviting your partner into your inner world, helping them better understand you. Some examples of authentic vulnerability include:

- **Sharing your feelings:** Expressing genuine emotions, such as fear, sadness, or insecurity, without hiding or minimizing them, for instance, saying, "I feel anxious about our future together, and I could use some support in working through it." This level of transparency encourages open communication and enables both partners to support each other through difficult times.
- **Being open and direct about your needs:** Communicating your needs and desires openly and directly, without manipulation or hidden agendas. For example, expressing, "I need more quality time together to feel connected and valued in our relationship" conveys your needs clearly and invites collaboration in finding solutions. This clear and honest communication encourages mutual understanding and strengthens the bond between the two of you.
- **Addressing imperfections:** Acknowledging your mistakes, flaws, and limitations with humility and honesty. Saying something like "I made a mistake, and I'm sorry. I take responsibility for my mistake, and I'm committed to making things right" shows you have accountability and integrity. When you take ownership of your actions and express genuine remorse or a commitment to improvement, you're setting a positive example for healthy conflict resolution and commitment to growth.

In contrast, manipulative vulnerability involves using emotional disclosures as a tactic for control, guilt-tripping, fishing for reassurance, or avoidance of responsibility. It often comes from a place of fear, insecurity, or a desire to elicit a specific response or action from your partner. While not always intentional, manipulative vulnerability can sometimes manifest as indirect or passive-aggressive communication aimed at coercing your partner into meeting your needs without explicitly stating them. For example:

- **Assuming the role of victim:** Portraying yourself as a victim to elicit sympathy or avoid accountability for your actions, for instance, saying, "I know I'm such a difficult, needy partner, and you could do so much better" in hopes of your partner reassuring you that isn't the case. This behavior can lead to an emotional imbalance in the relationship dynamics.
- **Emotional blackmail:** Leveraging your vulnerabilities or insecurities to manipulate your partner's behavior or decisions, for example, saying, "I feel sad when you go on friends' trips because I feel that if you really loved me, you wouldn't want to spend time with your friends instead of me." This can put unfair pressure on your partner and lead to them questioning or defending their feelings. Ultimately, this may lead to feelings of resentment, insecurity, and mistrust.
- **Withholding information:** Intentionally leaving out relevant details because of feelings of shame or embarrassment, for instance, expressing that you're stressed over finances but not disclosing to your partner you just splurged on something you didn't need. This omission could lead to misunderstandings and erode trust in the relationship, whereas sharing the information openly could foster understanding and strengthen communication.

Instead of resorting to—intentional or unintentional—manipulation, practice direct communication by clearly expressing your needs and desires to your partner. Rather than hinting at what you want or expecting your partner to read between the lines, openly articulate your expectations and boundaries. True intimacy flourishes when both partners feel safe to be their authentic selves and communicate openly and honestly.

KEEP THE FOCUS ON YOU, NOT THEM

When you decide to share about your anxiety, it's important to focus on yourself rather than on your partner. While it might feel like your anxiety is centered around your partner, it's not truly about them. It's about how your brain is processing, interpreting, and catastrophizing information related to them. In addition to being vulnerable, another way to decrease the likelihood of your partner's feelings being hurt or their getting defensive is to keep the focus of the conversation on you.

For example, instead of saying, "You've really been making me doubt our connection lately. Ever since you received your promotion, you've been traveling so much for work, and we hardly spend any time together. When you get home, you're withdrawn, and all you care about is going to bed. You're giving me anxiety because it makes me wonder if you even love me and if our relationship is going to work."

You could say, "I've been feeling less confident about our connection recently, especially with the increase in travel since your promotion. I understand how important this opportunity is for you, and I'm really proud of you. But I've noticed there has been more distance between us, both physically and emotionally, and it's been hard for me. When I asked myself why I feel this way, I realized it might be because of my parents' divorce. I remember how their relationship changed when one of them traveled frequently for work, and it's led me to worry about *our* future together. Sometimes I know these stories are not true, but other times it's harder to push them out of my head. When this happens, I can overanalyze or withdraw, and I don't want to do that because I love you. I just don't want our relationship to end up like my parents'."

Using "I" statements and sharing how you feel, rather than how your partner "makes you" feel, allows you to get the same point across with less risk of triggering defensiveness and hurt in your partner. Presenting information in this way paves the way for more connection and collaboration, while still providing space for you to share your truth and express your needs.

DON'T OVERSHARE DETAILS

When discussing relationship anxiety with your partner, remember that less can often be more. It is important to be honest and vulnerable, but avoid sharing too many details that might overwhelm you or your partner. Not because there is anything to be ashamed of in the details but rather to safeguard against compulsively oversharing, which will only reinforce your anxiety.

Rather than delving into the specific details of every thought and worry that consumes your mind, focus instead on expressing your general feelings and emotions in a way your partner can understand. The goal is less about getting reassurance and more about educating your partner on how they can support you effectively.

The anxiety-driven part of your brain may urge you to share every detail about every thought, but remember, that level of detail is not necessary for your partner to understand the essence of your relationship anxiety. Just because your anxiety insists you share something doesn't mean you must share it. As a reminder, you can't control the presence of your thoughts, but you can control whether or not you obey them. Before choosing whether or not to share something with your partner, it can be helpful to ask yourself some questions such as:

- Does my partner really need to know these details to understand the crux of my relationship anxiety?

- Does this information offer any value to my partner?
- Is knowing this information pertinent to the future of our relationship?
- Does sharing this information have greater potential to harm or help our connection?
- Is this important information for my partner to know, or is it a compulsive dump/vent to get this off my chest and feel relief?

For example, let's say you were attending a wedding and thought one of the servers was attractive. This could lead to questions like: "Am I being disloyal to my partner?" and "Would I be attracted to someone else if I truly loved my partner?" Later, when talking to your partner, you may feel compelled to say, "I found a server attractive tonight. I'm sorry, please forgive me." While technically true, your partner probably doesn't need to hear those details. Sharing that information would not offer your partner any value, it's not pertinent to the future of your relationship, it could potentially hurt their feelings, and while it would likely make you feel better in the moment to confess, it'd reinforce your confessing behaviors in the future.

Instead, you could say, "Sometimes, my anxiety gets triggered when we go out, and it's difficult to stay present. If it seems like I'm distracted, please know it's not that I don't want to be there; I just might be getting caught up in my head. If you notice, taking my hand or giving me a kiss could be helpful." Here, this information provides insight, value, and guidance for future moments of support and connection.

As another example, imagine you're wondering if you're with the right partner because your ex gave you more sentimental gifts than your current partner. Rather than sharing these exact details, you might say, "Sometimes my anxiety latches onto things that happened in the past, and I have a really hard time letting them go. This makes it difficult for me to focus on the present, and I start to doubt our connection." This provides insight into how relationship anxiety might affect you, without providing details that could cause unnecessary hurt.

It's important to recognize that while sharing your truth might occasionally hurt your partner's feelings, there's a distinction between expressing your needs and anxieties in the desire for growth and dumping your worries at the urging of anxiety to alleviate temporary discomfort. Your partner doesn't need to know every detail to understand, love, and support you.

TAKE PERSONAL ACCOUNTABILITY

Another valuable component to setting your conversations with your partner up for success is to let them know what you're doing to support yourself. Personal awareness and accountability play a crucial role in secure, healthy relationships. Let your partner know you are aware that many of your fears and doubts are a result of your anxiety, not true problems within your relationship. Reinforce the fact that your experience with relationship anxiety is particularly painful *because* you care about them and *because* the relationship is important to you, not the other way around.

You may consider sharing some specifics about what you've learned about relationship anxiety and the different ways it can show up. Maybe you could tell your partner about some aha moments or things that have become clear to you as you've learned more about relationship anxiety. As you feel comfortable, you could also consider sharing how you're making a commitment to work through your anxiety and what you're doing to support yourself. Sharing your goals and ideas for taking responsibility for your own anxiety recovery can help set your partner up for success in encouraging you and holding you accountable along the way. This may include letting them know you're:

- Reading this book.
- Working with a therapist or coach.
- Engaging in regular self-care.
- Trying out certain tools and techniques when you get triggered.

Letting your partner know you're taking ownership of your relationship anxiety takes the onus off of them to "fix" it and opens up space for them to be the supportive partner rather than the problem solver.

LET THEM KNOW HOW TO SUPPORT YOU

If you're able to tell your partner how relationship anxiety shows up for you, they will be better able to support your healing and avoid fueling your anxiety.

For example, your well-meaning partner may instinctively want to reassure you that your doubts are unfounded and your thoughts are not true and to assure you that they love you and care about you deeply. While that's relieving to hear, as you likely know by now the relief from those statements will be short-lived. Seeking certainty from your partner can be an enticing way to decrease your anxiety, but as discussed in Chapter 3, the constant need for validation can create a cycle of dependence and insecurity, increasing your anxiety in the long term. Rather than fueling the anxiety cycle through reassurance, your partner could instead gently remind you to prioritize self-care, encourage you to engage in activities that bring you joy, give you a hug or a kiss, or remind you how capable you are of tolerating discomfort and uncertainty.

When sharing with your partner, be clear and direct about your needs; they don't know how to best support you unless you let them know. The more honest you can be with them about which behaviors are keeping you stuck, the more supportive they can be. For instance:

- If you avoid social events due to anxiety, you might want your partner to encourage you to attend rather than supporting you in staying home.
- If you seek repeated reassurance, they could refrain from immediate responses rather than easing your doubts.

Some general ways you can encourage your partner to support you could include their:

- Suggesting a time-out on a conversation when you're overwhelmed with anxious thoughts.
- Reminding you that feelings will pass and that you've overcome challenges before.
- Encouraging new coping strategies when you fall into old patterns.
- Offering comfort or distraction when you're visibly upset.
- Acknowledging your progress and expressing pride in your efforts.
- Validating your feelings while gently challenging anxious thoughts.
- Reminding you to prioritize self-care and enjoyable activities.

The very act of opening up about your anxiety and receiving support from your partner can remind you they are by your side and committed to the relationship. Do your best to be clear about your needs, but understand that your partner may not always support you in the exact way you want. Ultimately your healing is your responsibility, and placing too much reliance on your partner can lead to disappointment and increased anxiety.

DON'T OVER-APOLOGIZE

People with relationship anxiety often apologize excessively to their partner. Whether it's for expressing needs, asking questions, sharing emotions, or simply existing with thoughts and doubts, many people with relationship anxiety find themselves constantly apologizing for every little thing. It's helpful to recognize that this behavior is not only unnecessary but can also have unintended effects on your relationship dynamics.

Consider how you feel when someone around you apologizes for *everything*. It's likely the apologies are excessive and leave you in an awkward position. In fact, you may have noticed that it can even sometimes be a bit annoying to hear someone apologize unnecessarily. Constantly saying you're sorry can lower your self-worth and sends the message to yourself—and others—that you're not deserving of love or acceptance.

Remember that your partner is with you because they love you, not because they expect you to apologize for existing. Instead of impulsively apologizing, try to cultivate confidence in yourself and your worthiness to take up space. Remind yourself it's okay to have needs, questions, emotions, doubts, and thoughts—these are all part of being human and being in a relationship. Apologize only when you really need to right a wrong.

By letting go of the habit of over-apologizing, you'll improve your self-esteem and enhance the quality of communication in your relationship. A healthy partner will appreciate your authenticity and confidence, and your connection will deepen as a result.

REMEMBER TO EXPRESS GRATITUDE

Expressing heartfelt gratitude at the end of a meaningful conversation is a valuable practice to adopt. To be well received, the appreciation must be genuine and authentic, so only share what feels true to you. You may consider thanking your partner for their time, energy, patience, insight, and/or support. If it feels authentic, you can also let them know how much you appreciate their willingness to have the conversation in the first place, understand your perspective, and create a safe, nonjudgmental space to share.

As you wrap up the conversation, you can also check in to see if your partner has any questions about what you've shared. Keep in mind that if a question feels too personal or triggers too much discomfort, it's okay to thank them for their curiosity but say you're not ready to address it at that moment. You can assure them that if and when you're ready to discuss it, you will let them know.

Through both expressing gratitude and encouraging open dialogue, you create space for growth and equality within your relationship. Keep in mind that even if the conversation doesn't unfold exactly as you planned, each step forward strengthens your connection. Deep trust, intimacy, and connection are built one step forward at a time.

> Case Study: Breaking the Pattern of Breaking Up

Sarah had a pattern of ending relationships whenever her doubts became too much to handle. Rather than risking sharing her feelings with previous partners, she would call it quits, hoping to find a more perfect partner she wouldn't have doubts about. However, when she found herself experiencing similar anxieties in her relationship with Alex, she made a conscious decision not to follow the same pattern. Instead of resorting to her usual response of breaking up, Sarah chose to lean into the discomfort and have a vulnerable conversation with Alex about her fears.

She mustered up the courage to share her feelings with Alex, admitting that she loved him deeply and didn't want to end their relationship but that sometimes her anxiety made her consider it. Opening up in this way felt terrifying yet liberating for Sarah, as she had never allowed herself to be so vulnerable with a partner before.

To her relief, Alex responded with compassion and a desire to better understand, assuring Sarah he valued their relationship just as much as she did. He listened to her concerns while trying to learn how he could help her feel more secure in the relationship.

As they navigated Sarah's anxiety together, they discovered a sense of closeness and connection. By checking in with one another regularly, they felt as though they were prioritizing the relationship and strengthening their bond. Over time, Sarah began to feel more secure in their relationship, knowing she could trust Alex to be there for her during difficult times and was able to relax into the present moment more frequently. Today, Sarah and Alex are thriving as a couple, their relationship stronger than ever before.

OVERCOMING RELATIONSHIP ANXIETY

IMPLEMENT STRATEGIES FOR CO-REGULATION

Co-regulation is the process whereby two individuals manage and soothe their emotional states together through shared activities, mutual support, and open communication. In the context of relationship anxiety, co-regulation involves partners working together to alleviate anxiety through creating a sense of safety and connection. While it can be uncomfortable to risk rocking the boat in your relationship, conquering challenges together can be a bonding activity and serve as a testament to the strength and resilience of your relationship. Whether it's working through a disagreement, overcoming an obstacle, or supporting each other through a personal challenge, every trial you face together is an opportunity to strengthen your bond and create deeper feelings of trust and intimacy. Remembering that your partner is on your side and inviting them to play a supportive role in your anxiety recovery journey can benefit both of you. Here are some ways to involve them in your healing process.

Celebrate Your Wins

In addition to acknowledging the fears, lows, and insecurities you're feeling within the relationship, it's equally important to celebrate the wins. Make a conscious effort to share with your partner the moments you feel closest and most secure. By addressing both the challenges and the celebrations head-on, you challenge the brain's all-or-nothing thinking and increase the likelihood of experiencing more confident and secure moments. Making a commitment to highlighting both the positive and the negative can also enhance feelings of trust within the relationship, demonstrating you're in it together through thick and thin.

Create Routines and Traditions

Establishing routines and traditions together can be a powerful way to strengthen your bond and serve as a reminder of the love and connection you share. Anxiety likes to have you thinking about the what-ifs, while routines can anchor you in the present moment and focus on what *is*, right now. Routines and traditions also put fun events on your calendar and bring your focus back to the things that are most important to you.

Whether it's a morning ritual of sharing coffee and conversation, a weekly date night, or an annual vacation to your favorite destination, these shared experiences can give you something to look forward to and serve as hallmarks of your relationship that ground you in moments of joy and unity.

Try Joint Activities, Too

Integrating co-regulation strategies into your daily or weekly routine can also enhance your bond and cultivate a sense of emotional connection and calmness. Practices such as partner yoga, partner dance, synchronized breathing, and singing or playing music together can help regulate and sync your nervous systems. These shared experiences help you relax and have fun together and set you up for a stronger emotional connection.

Schedule Regular Check-Ins

Scheduling conversations with your partner may not seem thrilling, but it can be a powerful practice for nurturing a healthy and connected relationship. In our fast-paced world, where schedules often dictate our time, setting aside time for heart-to-hearts ensures that the important stuff doesn't get lost in the shuffle. You can think of it as a standing date with your favorite person.

Scheduled check-ins also create a predictable and safe environment for sharing thoughts, feelings, and concerns without the pressure of spontaneity. It gives you the opportunity to check in on what is working and what needs to shift. By knowing when to expect these conversations, both partners can come prepared, ready to listen and share with intentionality and respect.

Keep in mind that these check-ins are not just for troubleshooting. They're also an opportunity to celebrate wins, big or small, and express gratitude for each other's presence in your lives.

Seek Outside Support

If you think it would help you and your partner, don't hesitate to seek outside support as you work through relationship anxiety. Counseling or coaching can provide personalized guidance and tools that are tailored to your needs. There is no shame in recognizing you need extra support—it's actually a sign of strength and commitment to your relationship!

If the prospect of seeking outside support feels overwhelming, take it one step at a time. Begin by having an open conversation with your partner about the type of support that would best suit the needs of you both. Consider options such as individual therapy, couples counseling, coaching, or attending a retreat together.

When exploring your options, prioritize the connection you feel with the provider. While the provider doesn't need to become your best friend, it's crucial to feel heard, validated, respected, and supported in your healing journey. Additionally, seek a provider who will appropriately challenge you and encourage you to shift patterns and behaviors that may be hindering your relationship's growth.

If you're unsure where to start looking and you have access to health insurance, consider utilizing resources available through your insurance provider or exploring recommendations included in the Resource List at the back of this book. Remember that various therapeutic styles and approaches exist, so take the time to find one that resonates with you and your partner. If you don't feel a strong connection with the first provider you meet with, don't be discouraged! Sometimes the first match isn't the right fit, and that's okay. Try to keep an open mind and be willing to try again with someone new when you're ready.

Once you find someone who's a good fit, do your best to be honest and open in your sessions. Your openness ensures that you receive individualized guidance aligned with your specific needs. Also, understand that investing your time and resources in therapy, coaching, or a retreat requires commitment and patience. Give the process a set period, such as a minimum of four sessions, before evaluating its effectiveness. Sometimes progress takes time to manifest, so be patient with yourself and the process before deciding it won't work for you.

Exercise:
Shared Journaling

Most people think of journaling as a solo activity, but it doesn't have to be. Making a journal with your partner can increase self-reflection and boost appreciation, intimacy, and connection by providing a platform for expressing thoughts, celebrating wins, and acknowledging each other's strengths. The journal itself could be a simple notebook or a DIY creation you make together. Follow these steps for shared journaling:

1. **Establish a routine:** Select one partner to write in the journal in the morning and the other in the evening.
2. **Set guidelines for entry sharing:** For example, spend five to ten minutes each day writing. Feel free to customize the sharing guidelines to suit your relationship dynamic. You could consider adding or removing prompts based on what you both find meaningful or adjusting the timing and frequency of entries to fit your schedules. Here are some example prompts:

   - I'm proud of myself for:
   - I'm proud of you for:
   - I'm proud of us for:
   - Something I'm working toward is:
   - A request I have is:

3. **Pass the journal:** When it's your turn to write, read your partner's previous entry with an open heart and mind, then share your own

responses to the prompts. If you wish to respond with words of encouragement or gratitude, do so under their entry.

4. **Respond and reflect:** Consider the thoughts your partner shared. Try to fulfill their requests whenever you can. Periodically, review your entries together as a couple, perhaps during a scheduled check-in.

Use this journal as an opportunity to reflect on your shared experiences, celebrate progress, practice being vulnerable, and discuss any patterns or insights that come up.

Key Takeaways

- Opening up to your partner about relationship anxiety can strengthen your bond, but it's essential to choose the right time and mindset for these conversations. Being vulnerable and expressing your feelings directly and authentically can lead to deeper understanding and empathy.
- Be mindful of the level of details you share about your thoughts and feelings. Avoid compulsive oversharing; instead, ask yourself whether the information you're sharing is pertinent to the relationship's health and longevity or merely venting to alleviate temporary discomfort.
- While you're responsible for your own healing, you and your partner are a team. Celebrating your wins together; co-regulating through movement, music, or breathwork; creating meaningful traditions; and/or seeking outside support as necessary can help you feel like you're in it together, bringing you closer as partners.

CHAPTER 11

GRIEVING AND MOVING FORWARD

On the journey to overcoming relationship anxiety, there comes a pivotal moment where you must confront all that anxiety has taken from your life. The people, opportunities, experiences, and dreams lost to the relentless grip of anxiety may be accompanied by deep grief. Like any loss, your grief deserves to be acknowledged, felt, processed, and accepted to the best of your ability.

This chapter will cover the complexities of grief in anxiety, explain the sunk cost fallacy, and show you how to work toward self-forgiveness—all of which can help pave the way toward healing and growth. You'll learn how grief is the process of letting go not just of what tangible things have been lost but also of the dreams that will never be realized. Lastly, it will highlight how grief is a universal experience, a bittersweet acknowledgment that life continuously moves forward, carrying with it not only the weight of what could have been but also the possibility of all that still can be. This hope can help carry you forward into your new future.

RECOGNIZE THE TOLL ANXIETY TAKES ON YOUR LIFE

As you learn more about relationship anxiety, it can often lead you down paths of introspection, where you face the many ways anxiety has impacted your life. There's no way to sugarcoat it: It's sobering to look back and recognize how much of your precious time and how many of your opportunities, experiences, and relationships have been overshadowed by—or completely lost to—anxiety.

If you have this realization, it's natural to find yourself mourning not only what is no longer but also what could have been. You might replay scenarios in your mind, imagining alternate realities where anxiety didn't hold power over your thoughts and actions. Perhaps you wonder what life could have been like if a relationship had lasted, if you had known then what you know now, or if you had been able to pursue opportunities without the heavy burden of anxiety weighing you down.

Thinking of All the What-Ifs

How many people and experiences have you walked away from out of fear? How many relationships did your anxiety prevent you from being present to? How many relationships did you endure for far too long, afraid to call them off for fear of being alone or making the wrong decision? How many hours of your life could have been spent in alignment with your values rather than consumed by obsessive thoughts and compulsive behaviors?

These losses are real, tangible, and deserving of recognition. In acknowledging these losses, it's important to recognize that this process is not about dwelling on the past indefinitely or wallowing in regret. Rather, it's about validating your experiences and allowing yourself the space to heal.

Please know that the weight of these losses isn't something you have to carry with you for the rest of your life. By acknowledging the impact that anxiety has had on your life, you give yourself permission to honor the pain and suffering you've endured. This acknowledgment is a crucial step on the path to healing, as it allows you to work toward releasing the past and to embrace the possibility of a happier future. Healing is not about erasing the past but rather about moving forward by taking the next best step possible, regardless of what happened in the past.

Similar to an anxiety spiral, in your grief you may find yourself preoccupied with endless what-if scenarios, replaying past events in a futile attempt to make sense of it all. But dwelling on these what-ifs only serves to keep you stuck in an anxious and obsessive cycle. It rarely helps you change your current situation and instead prevents you from fully engaging with your current situation and moving forward with your life. To honor and process the grief of what anxiety has taken from your life while taking tangible steps toward moving forward, consider incorporating practices that promote healing and self-reflection rather than practices that lead to your dwelling in regret.

Exercise:
Grieving What Was Lost to Anxiety

Acknowledging what has been lost to your anxiety can be a powerful step along your journey to overcoming relationship anxiety. In the upcoming week, consider setting aside some time and space to grieve and incorporate one or more of the following options into your schedule. If these ideas do not resonate, feel free to grieve, process, or memorialize your loss(es) in whichever way feels most authentic to you. You may find it helpful to:

- Write a tribute to a previous version of yourself, recognizing the resilience and strength you've demonstrated in the face of adversity.
- Write a love letter or apology letter to your past self to help foster self-compassion and forgiveness, offering closure and acceptance.
- Memorialize this period of your life in some way, whether through journaling, creating art, or compiling a scrapbook of meaningful memories.
- Reconnect with the dreams and aspirations lost to anxiety and re-commit to those that are still achievable as a way to focus on the future.
- Engage in acts of service, such as spreading awareness, volunteering, or contributing to fundraisers, as a way of providing a sense of ful-fillment and connection to others.

- Consider framing a photo of yourself at a younger age, symbolizing the journey of growth and transformation, and honor that version of yourself by embracing uncertainty and facing your fears with courage and resilience each day.

These practices can serve as powerful tools for processing grief, fostering self-compassion, and reclaiming autonomy over your life.

GRIEF IS UNAVOIDABLE

While no one wants to feel grief, it is an unavoidable part of the human experience, touching us all at various points in our lives. It doesn't just stem from tragic events; it arises from the very act of making decisions. Every decision we make involves trade-offs, and with each choice, there may be a sense of loss for the paths not taken. Whether you commit to a relationship, embrace singlehood, pursue a career, or embark on a new adventure, you inevitably grieve the possibilities left behind. In choosing one life path, you may grieve the potential life paths not lived.

Normalizing the experience of grief—without attaching judgment or shame to it—is crucial, especially when navigating relationship anxiety. It's important to recognize that experiencing grief doesn't inherently mean you've made the wrong decision or that you're unhappy with your current circumstances.

Many individuals with relationship anxiety harbor fears of making the wrong choices in their relationship and facing potential heartbreak, boredom, or disappointment in the future. The uncertainty of what lies ahead may overwhelm you with fear, leading to a reluctance to fully invest in relationships or pursue your dreams.

However, accepting the inevitability of grief can free you from the grip of fear and allow you to live authentically in the present. While it's very human to worry about being hurt or experiencing loss, avoiding love or commitment in an attempt to shield yourself from pain only deprives you of the joy and depth of the human experience. If something unfortunate were to happen in your relationship, you would grieve. Your heart would hurt *and* you would learn to cope and move forward.

Learning to embrace grief—for what has happened, what hasn't happened, and what may happen—is an essential aspect of healing and growth. It's an acknowledgment of the intricacies of life and a recognition of your capacity to feel deeply and face adversity with resilience and adaptability. When you practice confronting your grief head-on, you may discover profound insights about yourself and the world around you. You will learn to cultivate deeper compassion, both for yourself and for others, and you can learn to refocus on controlling what is within your control while releasing what isn't.

Rather than dwelling on what-ifs and what-could-have-beens, you can choose to focus on the present moment and trust in your ability to handle whatever challenges come your way, if/when they come your way. By embracing the full spectrum of human emotion, including grief, you open yourself up to a deeper sense of love, connection, purpose, and fulfillment.

MANAGE REAL-TIME GRIEF

Recognizing what anxiety has taken from your life doesn't only apply to past relationships or experiences; it can also manifest as a very real, present-day struggle within your current relationship. For example, you might long to have the desire for sexual intimacy with your partner but find it challenging due to anxiety-induced factors like decreased libido from chronic stress, worries about appearance or performance, insecurity around pleasing your partner, physical pain, or being mentally preoccupied with anxious or intrusive thoughts whenever the opportunity presents itself.

This real-time deprivation caused by anxiety can evoke profound feelings of frustration, sadness, inadequacy, and even anger. Feeling left out while hearing about others' fulfilling sex lives only serves to exacerbate these emotions, intensifying the sense of isolation and longing. Yet, paradoxically, the more you want to want it, the less turned on you might feel.

Recognizing this form of real-time grief within a relationship is important. Like all grief, it deserves to be felt and validated. Discussing real-time grief, whether it's around intimacy or another aspect of the relationship, can feel uncomfortable. Still, opening up to your partner about these challenges can increase understanding, provide a safe space to grieve, and ultimately help you move forward toward your relationship goals.

PROCESS TRAUMA AND ANGER

The more you reflect on how intense life with relationship anxiety can feel at times, the more you might recognize the profound impact it has had on so many different aspects of your life. It's not just about feeling nervous before a date or second-guessing a text message. It's about the relentless toll it takes on your mental and emotional well-being, leaving you feeling exhausted, defeated, and, sometimes, alone even when you're in a loving relationship.

For some people, relationship anxiety can even be a traumatic experience. At its peak, relationship anxiety can feel like you're trapped in a never-ending cycle of doubt and fear, where even the simplest interactions can trigger overwhelming feelings of panic and insecurity. It can feel like a constant battle against your own mind, feeling like you've lost control of it—thoughts and emotions swarming against your will. At times this can leave you feeling helpless, hopeless, and alone.

This is often one of the most challenging aspects of dealing with relationship anxiety: the feeling of powerlessness that accompanies it.

For many, it can feel like no matter how hard they try, they can't seem to escape the grip of their own thoughts and fears. This loss of control can be incredibly destabilizing, leaving you feeling consumed by uncertainty and doubt.

If this is you as you confront the impact and/or trauma of relationship anxiety, it's natural to experience a range of emotions, including anger. You might feel anger at:

- Yourself for not being able to "just stop worrying."
- Your present or past partners for not understanding what you're going through.
- The world for being so unfair—why do you have to be dealing with this in the first place!?
- Yourself for all the relationships you sabotaged due to having anxiety or all the times you micromanaged, rejected, or lashed out at a partner in a state of panic and uncertainty.
- The fact that people were hurt by your anxiety along the way.

This anger is a valid response to the pain and suffering you've endured, and like with sadness, it's important to acknowledge it in healthy ways rather than suppressing it. After all, anger is a natural and expected part of most grieving and healing processes. It is an outward expression of your inner turmoil, a reflection of the deep-seated frustration and resentment you feel toward anxiety and its impact on your life. Many times when you're feeling angry toward yourself, your partner, or your relationship, you might actually be feeling angry toward your anxiety.

As with all emotions, keep in mind that your anger will be transient. It might be a necessary part of the healing process, but it's not the end destination. By acknowledging your anger and allowing yourself to feel it fully—without judging yourself for having it—you can begin to release the grip it holds on you.

Stages of Grief

In her book *On Death and Dying*, Dr. Elisabeth Kübler-Ross shared that the five stages of grief include denial, anger, bargaining, depression, and acceptance. To better reflect the complexities of grief, more recent models expand on these initial five to include stages such as shock, relief, guilt, and reconstruction. You can experience some—or all—of these at different phases as you grieve in your own life. Do your best to give yourself grace and know that grief is a very personal journey.

AVOID THE SUNK COST FALLACY

The sunk cost fallacy is a way of describing the mindset that leads people to make decisions based on past investments rather than objectively evaluating their current situation. In the realm of relationship anxiety, the sunk cost fallacy can trap you in relationships that no longer serve you. You might convince yourself that because of all the time, effort, and emotions you've already invested in your relationship, you must continue to invest in it, regardless of whether it's bringing you happiness or aligns with your current needs and values.

This Mindset Keeps You Stuck

You might cling to the familiar, fearing the uncertainty of change and convincing yourself that you can't possibly walk away. You might believe you've put in too much effort helping your partner grow and change that if you walk away, they will be a great partner for someone else instead of you. You might believe that you are too old to start over or that all the "good ones" are off the market so you should stick with what you have.

One of the main issues with this mindset is that you're investing time and energy in a misaligned relationship out of the (often baseless) hope it will eventually improve and one day become aligned.

Remember our discussion in Chapter 2 about settling. There is a difference between choosing to settle with a great, if imperfect, partner and choosing to stay in a toxic or unfulfilling relationship out of fear, guilt, or obligation. Rationalizing the decision to stay in a relationship that's wrong for you based on future potential disregards the toll it's taking on your mental and emotional well-being in the present.

Putting Yourself First

Breaking free from the sunk cost fallacy requires a shift in mindset—a willingness to prioritize your happiness and self-respect over the length of your relationship. It involves recognizing that past investments, while significant, should not dictate your future decisions. Instead, try to focus on making value-based choices that align with your current goals and relationship vision and learn to grieve the losses that may come with it. These losses may include that of your partner, their potential, and/or the life you imagined the two of you could have together but never did and never will. Sometimes we cling to the fantasy of what our relationship was or could be rather than the reality of what it actually is. Sometimes you'll need to grieve not only the person but also the version of the person you thought they were. The version you *hoped* they were. By giving yourself permission to grieve in this way, you can also give yourself permission to embrace the freedom that comes with accepting reality and moving forward.

THE VARIOUS SOURCES OF RELATIONSHIP GRIEF

In the context of relationships, grief arises from various sources. There are the more obvious sources, such as the death of a loved one or end of a partnership. But grief can also stem from experiences in ongoing relationships, such as a loss of independence, change of routine, physical relocation, or simply growing and maturing into a new phase of life. For example:

- You might be excited to move in with your partner while simultaneously grieving the flexibility and autonomy of living alone.
- You might be entering into parenthood and be thrilled to start a new phase of life while simultaneously grieving aspects of your pre-parent life.
- You might be happy you met your partner later in life at a time when you're clearer about your needs and values while simultaneously grieving the fact that you'll never experience your wild and carefree early twenties with them.

It's important to validate these emotions while also recognizing that grieving certain aspects of a relationship doesn't diminish the love or commitment shared. This highlights the power of "both/and" thinking, where you can experience seemingly contradictory emotions simultaneously. In the examples provided, both emotions can coexist without invalidating each other. For instance, grieving the loss of flexibility in living alone alongside the excitement of moving in with a partner doesn't necessarily imply moving in together was the wrong choice. Instead, it might signal the need to prioritize flexibility in this new phase of life while still embracing the decision to move in together.

PROCESSING GRIEF REQUIRES SELF-COMPASSION AND SELF-FORGIVENESS

Self-compassion and self-forgiveness are essential components to help you embrace this spectrum of emotions. In times of pain and uncertainty—which are common hallmarks of grief—it's common to be self-critical, especially when faced with loss and regret. However, practicing self-compassion involves extending kindness and understanding to yourself, acknowledging you've done the best you could with the resources available to you at any given moment.

Embracing self-compassion won't erase your grief, but it can create a supportive inner monologue that encourages acceptance, warmth, and confidence alongside your grief. Tell yourself that for every moment you spend dwelling on past regrets, you'll spend an equal amount celebrating your progress, no matter how small. Remember that your victories—no matter how trivial you think they are—are significant milestones along your unique journey.

Similarly, self-forgiveness plays a crucial role in releasing the burdens of guilt and shame. Understand that holding onto past mistakes only hinders your ability to move forward. Try your best to embrace forgiveness as a gift to yourself, a way of freeing yourself from regret and self-blame.

Forgiving yourself doesn't mean minimizing or excusing anyone's past actions; it is simply acknowledging them with compassion and understanding. Do your best to recognize that you are human—flawed and fallible yet inherently worthy of love and acceptance. Allow yourself the grace to learn from your experiences and grow into a stronger, more resilient version of yourself rather than holding yourself in contempt for the rest of your life.

While practicing self-compassion and self-forgiveness may be easier said than done, incorporating them into your daily life will bring some relief. As you cultivate these qualities, you create space for healing and transformation, reclaiming your power from anxiety. Embrace your imperfections as integral parts of your healing journey and remember that self-compassion and self-forgiveness truly are signs of strength, not weakness. They allow you to embrace your humanity with humility and grace, which ultimately leads to greater connection, both within yourself and with your partner.

> Case Study: No More Relationships Lost to Anxiety

After a series of failed relationships and a particularly tumultuous breakup, William decided to seek therapy to better understand his patterns and behaviors. There he learned about relationship anxiety and how it can manifest in thoughts and behaviors that undermine trust and intimacy.

As he learned more about relationship anxiety, William began to reflect on his past relationships and realized how much his anxiety had impacted them. In particular, he thought back to a relationship he had a few years ago with Paul, a man he deeply cared about. Despite that care, he used to obsess over every interaction with Paul, fearing that he wasn't good enough for Paul and that Paul would eventually leave him. He struggled to communicate his feelings and needs, often withdrawing emotionally to avoid vulnerability. Eventually, communication broke down to the point where they decided to go their separate ways.

As William reflected on his time with Paul, he couldn't help but grieve and dwell on the what-ifs. He wondered if things would have been different if he had recognized his anxiety earlier and sought help. He questioned whether he had missed out on a chance at true happiness because of his fears and insecurities.

William grieved for all the ways anxiety had impacted his life. While there was a part of him that wanted to beat himself up for his past behavior, he realized that dwelling on the past was not productive. Instead, he committed to working through his anxiety and learning healthier ways to manage his doubts and fears so his current relationship didn't suffer the same fate. William began practicing self-compassion and non-engagement when his worries and doubts got the best of him.

Key Takeaways

- Relationship anxiety can lead to profound losses, including missed opportunities, strained relationships, and unfulfilled dreams. It's important to validate these losses, acknowledge the range of emotions that surfaces, and allow yourself the space to grieve and process the impact of anxiety on your life.

- The sunk cost fallacy can trap you in relationships that no longer serve you, leading to prolonged unhappiness and dissatisfaction. Prioritize personal happiness and growth over past investments to bring more clarity to your relationship decisions.
- Regardless of the paths you take and choices you make, you will experience grief. Grief is an inescapable aspect of life arising from various sources, such as loss, change, and decision-making. By accepting the inevitability of grief and practicing self-compassion and forgiveness, you can navigate the complexities of relationship anxiety with greater resilience, clarity, and purpose.

CHAPTER 12

REDEFINING RELATIONSHIP SUCCESS

Have you ever encountered something in life that didn't initially capture your heart yet with time became something cherished? Perhaps it's a family tradition you once begrudgingly participated in as a child but now eagerly anticipate every year. Or consider the cat scratches on your furniture or dog hair on your clothes that once frustrated you and now you hold as dear memories of your best furry friend. Life has a remarkable way of surprising us with beauty and joy, sometimes hidden behind our initial perceptions. Similarly, relationships often unfold in unpredictable ways.

While the risk of opening your heart may seem daunting, it's part of human nature to seek out relationships. Why? Because beyond the uncertainty lies the possibility of meaningful connection, security, and love. In this chapter, you will explore how relationships are a choice. Whether you choose to pursue a romantic relationship, "play the field," or remain in singlehood, each path comes with risks and rewards. We'll delve into what it means to be successful in a relationship and how choosing to be all in can be a better choice than sitting on the fence. Finally, this chapter serves to remind you of how capable and deserving you are of love and compassion, both within yourself and within a relationship.

DISCOVER YOUR PERSONAL DEFINITION OF RELATIONSHIP SUCCESS

We're often conditioned to believe that a successful relationship is one that follows a linear trajectory: meeting, falling in love, overcoming an obstacle or two, and then riding off into the sunset, hand in hand in perpetual bliss. But what does success in a relationship truly mean to *you*?

- Is it measured by the number of years spent together or the quality of those years?
- Is it measured by never disagreeing or by feeling safe and secure enough to speak up and risk disagreement?
- Is it measured by constant feelings of love and attraction or by a commitment to navigating the emotional highs and lows as a team toward a shared relationship vision?

Consider a relationship that lasts for decades but is marred by disconnection, resentment, or repeated toxic behavior. Is this truly a success? Conversely, consider one that's filled with connection, compassion, and love, but both partners decide it's best to part ways after a while. Is this really a failure? In a society that romanticizes longevity but sometimes overlooks the depth of connection, it can be enticing to prioritize the duration of your relationship and your feelings of love above all else. Yet the truth is, success in relationships is not defined by a single metric but rather a myriad of factors.

Relationships are as diverse and complex as the individuals within them. As such, a successful relationship can take on a multitude of forms, defined by your own personal goals and values. Success is not solely defined by feelings of love, the absence of conflict, or the longevity of a partnership. It's about the depth of connection, the mutual support of one another's goals and dreams, the commitment to growing both individually and together, the meaningful experiences shared, and the evolution that unfolds over time. It's about creating a safe space where both partners feel seen, heard, and valued for who they truly are. It's about weathering storms as a team, embracing vulnerability, disagreeing with curiosity and respect, and continually checking in with both yourself and your partner to ensure you're still sharing the same relationship vison.

Success in relationships also involves advocating for yourself, maintaining self-respect, and recognizing when it may be time to part ways. It's about honoring your morals, values, and boundaries, even if that means making difficult decisions.

As such, when considering whether or not you're in a successful relationship, ask yourself questions such as:

- Am I staying true to my values?
- Am I proud of the person I'm becoming in this relationship?
- Am I learning and growing in this relationship?
- Do I feel safe, supported, and encouraged in this relationship?
- Do I genuinely enjoy being around my partner the vast majority of the time?
- Do we navigate conflict together with respect and compassion?

While this is not an exhaustive list of questions to check in with, questions such as these can help you define the success of your relationship with more clarity and accuracy than asking yourself, "How long have we been together?" or "How in love do I feel today?"

When it comes to relationship anxiety, amid the intense feelings of uncertainty and doubt, a successful relationship may merely be defined as one you give yourself full permission to experience. Rather than spending months—or years—with one foot in the relationship and one foot out, try to decide if the relationship has what it takes to be successful, make a choice, and go all in. Success could be as simple as trusting yourself to make a wholehearted decision.

RELATIONSHIPS ARE A CHOICE

Relationships are not passive partnerships; they are active choices you make every day. Whether you choose to enter a relationship, leave a relationship, or linger in uncertainty, each decision carries its own weight, risk, and consequences.

Staying in a relationship comes with its joys and hardships and requires commitment, dedication, and risk. It means investing your time, energy, and emotions into nurturing the bond you share with your partner. It also entails sacrificing other potential paths and opportunities that may lie outside your current relationship. It's a conscious decision to prioritize what you have with your partner over the what-ifs and maybes that could exist elsewhere.

Choosing to leave a relationship comes with its own joys and hardships too. It requires grieving, rebuilding, and also risk. It entails letting go of the comfort and familiarity you've built over time, the shared memories, inside jokes, and moments of intimacy. It's a leap into uncertain new territory, fueled by the belief that your partner isn't an aligned fit, that you would prefer to be single, and/or that something better may be waiting for you.

The Problem with "One Foot In, One Foot Out"

Perhaps the most problematic choice of all is the one foot in, one foot out approach. It's a dance of indecision—a refusal to fully commit or let go. This mindset leads to a sense of perpetual limbo, where neither partner feels fully satisfied or fulfilled.

When one foot is tentatively dipped into the relationship while the other remains ready for the exit, a constant state of emotional flux results. This ambivalence breeds insecurity, as neither partner feels secure in the commitment or direction of the relationship. This erodes trust, intimacy, and feelings of closeness—the opposite of what you're looking for in a secure, loving partnership.

The one foot in, one foot out approach often stems from a fear of making the wrong decision. It's usually driven by a desire to avoid discomfort and uncertainty at all costs, even if that means sacrificing the potential for a great relationship. By keeping one foot firmly planted outside the relationship, you might believe you can maintain a sense of control over your future and protect yourself from potential heartache. You might be trying to convince yourself that you're in the safe position of being able to either commit or bolt as needed at any time. However, in reality this approach *increases* your likelihood of potential heartache. By holding yourself back from fully embracing the relationship, vulnerability and connection are often replaced by guardedness and self-protection. These undermine the depth, play, connection, and fulfillment that come with wholehearted commitment.

Your anxiety might trick you into thinking you're incapable of making a choice. It leads you to believe you can't tolerate big emotions, unexpected hurdles, or giving up control. It tries to convince you that you do not know what choice to make and/or that you can't handle the potential discomfort that comes along with the choice.

And yet, your anxiety is wrong. You have proven time and time again that you possess what it takes to handle life's uncertainties.

So, for better or worse, make a choice—a deliberate, intentional choice. Trust yourself enough to choose the path that aligns with your values, desires, and aspirations, knowing that *any* path you choose will come with risk and consequences. Trust that you have the courage and resourcefulness to make it through the inevitable imperfections and uncertainties that lie ahead. And most importantly, trust that you have the power to course correct if needed, without needing to figure out right now exactly how you'll do that. In trusting your judgment and taking calculated risks, you build confidence and clarity, regardless of the outcome.

SLOWING DOWN CAN HELP YOU FIND RELATIONSHIP SUCCESS

One of the greatest gifts you can give yourself as you navigate life with relationship anxiety is to slow down. Anxiety has a way of nudging us to speed through life, trying to fast-forward past moments of discomfort or uncertainty. It can feel like a force compelling you to put your head down and power through, hoping to avoid the weight of anxious thoughts. Micromanaging and overanalyzing become the norm as you seek to steer through life's challenges as quickly as possible. But at this hurried pace, what you're actually escaping are the moments that build true connection and joy—not escaping anxiety.

You might be looking forward to an event for months, only to catch yourself thinking, "I just can't wait until this is over" or "I wish this had already passed" once the event finally arrives. These thoughts, driven by what's called anticipatory anxiety, can feel draining and burdensome, pulling you away from the present moment and replacing an event you were looking forward to with one you dread. For example, if you have an anniversary celebration planned, anxiety may lead you to fixate on ways things could go wrong, causing you to dread the event rather than looking forward to it.

Oddly, having a sense of urgency is often a sign you need to slow down. Rather than rushing through life, take time to experience all the highs, the lows, and the mundane moments with your partner. As you embrace the full spectrum of emotions and experiences, knowing that some will exceed your expectations and some will fall short, you'll continue to learn that the success of your relationship is not made or broken by single interactions but by many life experiences over time. Neither you nor your partner has to be perfect for you both to be happy, and giving yourself the space and time to slowly, and fully, experience your relationship can help you create more meaningful experiences together.

GRANT YOUR PARTNER—AND YOURSELF— THE BENEFIT OF THE DOUBT

How you choose to take your partner's actions profoundly influences the dynamics of your relationship. It's easy to fall into a cycle of negativity, scrutinizing every action and assigning negative meanings to them. However, embracing the practice of giving your partner the benefit of the doubt can be transformative.

Granting your partner the benefit of the doubt doesn't mean overlooking major red flags or deal-breakers. It's about reframing your perspective, resisting the urge to magnify minor issues, and creating a space for curiosity and understanding.

Self-Compassion Will Benefit Your Partner Too

At the same time, extending kindness and compassion to yourself is equally vital. Those who are hard on their partners often hold themselves to similarly high standards. While granting your partner the benefit of the doubt is crucial for fostering trust and understanding in a relationship, it's essential to extend that same kindness and compassion to yourself. Remember, one of the most loving acts you can offer your partner is prioritizing self-nurturing and self-compassion.

Focusing on your own self-care and fulfillment means showing up for yourself in the same way you desire your partner to show up for you. If you'd like your partner to show you love, practice showing love to yourself. If you desire to be turned on in the bedroom, practice turning yourself on. If you'd like to be praised and celebrated, praise and celebrate yourself. While self-nurturing isn't a direct replacement for receiving love and validation from your partner, it enriches your well-being and creates a foundation for more supportive and positive exchanges with your partner.

In a healthy relationship, both partners contribute to each other's happiness and quality of life. However, it's essential to recognize that each individual is ultimately responsible for their own healing and coping mechanisms. Expecting your partner to cater to your insecurities, tiptoe around your triggers, or change to fit your idealized image of them is an act of control, not love. While leaning on your partner for support is a component of a healthy relationship, self-nurturing can help you stay in your lane and fill your own tank, without relying too heavily on your partner to "make you" happy.

Be Emotionally Generous

Your energy and intention have a huge impact on how you view your relationship. As discussed throughout this book, if you constantly focus on feelings of dissatisfaction or unappreciation, you're more likely to find evidence that reinforces these feelings. Take a moment to ask yourself if you are more consistently giving your partner the benefit of the doubt or if you are defaulting to assuming the worst.

In the case of genuine concerns that go beyond offering the benefit of the doubt, do your best to voice these concerns as directly and compassionately as possible. Stand up for what you want and need, and then be open to receiving. If your partner is receptive and does their best to implement your request, do your best to avoid squashing their efforts with criticism or micromanagement. Instead, try to acknowledge your partner's efforts to implement your requests as acts of love and consideration. Even if their efforts aren't perfect, appreciating their intentions and willingness increases feelings of closeness and the likelihood they will continue to work on this in the future. Criticizing their attempts at change may deter future efforts and hinder relationship growth.

Micromanaging or nitpicking can derail everyone's best efforts. For instance, imagine you've told your partner you love receiving surprise flowers, but lilies aren't your favorite. (You have this conversation in passing, mentioning it as a casual preference without much emphasis.) One day, your partner surprises you with a beautiful bouquet of assorted flowers, but nestled within them is a single lily. Instantly, you feel a mix of emotions: appreciation for the gesture mixed with disappointment they overlooked your preference.

Your mind beings to race with questions: "Do they not remember our conversation? Did they just choose the first bouquet they saw? Do they even care about what I want and like?" Suddenly, what was meant to be a thoughtful gesture feels like a negative, and you're left feeling hurt and misunderstood.

In the midst of these emotions, you have a choice in how to respond. You could express your disappointment with criticism, such as saying, "Thanks, but why did you get a bouquet with a lily? I told you I don't like lilies." This could potentially lead to defensiveness, hurt feelings, and a decrease in your partner's motivation to surprise you with flowers in the future.

Alternatively, you could choose to express gratitude for the gesture. Imagine responding with "Thank you so much for the beautiful bouquet. It means a lot that you remembered I love receiving flowers." Or, if not receiving lilies is particularly important to you, you may say something like "Thank you so much for the beautiful bouquet. It means a lot that you remembered I love receiving flowers. You may not have caught this because I mentioned it in passing, but for future reference, I'm not a fan of lilies. They're beautiful, but their strong smell gives me a headache. Luckily, I can easily pull the lily out, and the rest of the flowers smell great. Thanks again for thinking of me!"

By acknowledging the effort and thoughtfulness behind the gesture while also kindly expressing your preference, you open the door to constructive communication and maintain a connection with your partner, setting the foundation for similar positive exchanges in the future.

AVOID THE BACKDOOR SPIKE

Just as feelings will ebb and flow throughout your relationship, so too will your anxiety. As you continue to work toward overcoming the grip of anxiety over your life and relationship, it can be helpful to be aware of a phenomenon called the backdoor spike. This occurs when you're feeling less triggered and less anxious, but you start to get anxious that you're *not* feeling anxious.

Remember that your brain prefers what's familiar, so change, even positive change, can feel jarring at first. You might notice a few days or a few weeks of peace: moments when you're fully present without analyzing your partner, an evening when you forget to assess your feelings or compatibility, or a conversation that you don't rehash in your mind. Surprisingly, this act of forgetting to be anxious can make you feel anxious! If you experience this, it's essential to recognize that this is a positive sign of growth and healing in overcoming your relationship anxiety, and it's important for you to do your best not to retroactively analyze or check for feelings.

Instead, remind yourself that feeling less anxious is an indication you're utilizing new coping skills and strategies, living your values, and tolerating uncertainty. Rather than sliding back into anxiety, celebrate this progress and be proud of yourself! Remember, you've worked hard to reach this point, and getting here is a testament to your resilience and determination. Embrace this feeling as part of your healing process; don't fight against what you've been working so hard to achieve.

Anxiety Will Ebb and Flow

Similarly, there may be times when you feel like you've overcome your anxiety only for it to resurface unexpectedly. During these moments, it's natural to feel discouraged and as though you're back where you started. However, it's important to understand that experiencing setbacks is part of the healing process. It doesn't mean you've deviated from the healing path; it's simply a pitstop on the road to recovery.

During these challenging times where your anxiety resurfaces, consider revisiting your coping skills; spending quality time with friends, family, and/or animals; reflecting on what's happening in your life; or seeking support from a therapist or coach. While there isn't always an identifiable reason why your anxiety is resurfacing, many times it spikes in response to transitions, changes to routine, or new paths in life.

For example, before booking a big couples' trip six months out, your anxiety may resurface, wondering what will happen if you break up before then. Before a family reunion with relatives you haven't seen in years, your anxiety may resurface, wondering what people will think about your partner. At a friend's wedding, your anxiety may resurface, wondering if you're as in love and compatible as they are. In these moments, remind yourself that new experiences often trigger old patterns. You are still in charge of your actions. You still have a choice as to whether or not you side with your anxiety or with your values.

This could be a time to nurture yourself, communicate with your partner, and trust that this phase is temporary. Remember, all emotions are temporary, and feeling anxious doesn't negate the progress you've made or the beautiful moments you've shared with your partner.

As you continue to navigate life with relationship anxiety, do your best to embrace the peace in the moments you are content and ride the waves of tough times as smoothly as possible. Keep pushing through, knowing you are capable of both enjoying the beautiful moments and overcoming the challenging ones.

YOU *CAN'T* KNOW FOR SURE

A lingering question when it comes to relationship anxiety is often, "But how can I be *sure?*" Simply put, you can't. Fortunately, certainty isn't a prerequisite for a secure and fulfilling relationship. What's essential are vulnerability, confidence, and trust in both yourself and your partner.

When you find yourself wavering, or stuck in the one foot in, one foot out approach, consider what's known as a relational reckoning. Coined by relationship expert Terry Real, this concept involves a self-intervention where you ask yourself, "Am I receiving enough in this relationship to justify grieving what I'm not receiving?" Essentially, does the greatness of this relationship outweigh the pain caused by its imperfections? If your answer is yes, and you choose to stay, do so with confidence, gratitude, and an open heart. But if you find yourself unable to stay without lingering resentment, bitterness, or a desire to control your partner, it's worth asking yourself, "Why am I remaining in a relationship where I continuously feel resentful and bitter?"

Another similar approach is to ask yourself, "Do I have enough information to leave this relationship today?" If the answer is yes, then consider ending the relationship or reflecting on why you're hesitating to do so. If the answer is no, you do not have enough information to decide your partner is *not* for you, so stay. But commit fully: Stay with both feet in until you're clear you'd like to take both feet out.

For instance, imagine your partner is wonderful—you share similar life goals and values, and you feel safe and supported with them. However, they may not pay as much attention to sentimental details as you'd like. Is it ideal to be with someone who picks up on subtle hints and showers you with thoughtful surprises? Maybe. But does this flaw outweigh the strengths of the relationship? Only you can decide this for yourself. If you deem it a deal-breaker, trust your judgment and accept the consequences. If not, trust that your decision to stay is valid and work toward releasing resentment and focusing on what you are getting rather than fixating on what's lacking.

Remember, no relationship is perfect. There's a distinction between wanting your partner to be different and being unable to lead a fulfilling life with them as they are. Occasional hurt, grief, disappointment, and boredom are inevitable. All relationships come with risk, and the more potential for a future you see with your partner, the higher the stakes may feel. Keep in mind that yes, you're risking potential hurt but also the possibility of love, happiness, companionship, support, and security in partnership.

> Case Study: A Wonderful Man in an Awful Hat

Sheila and her husband, Leonardo, embarked on a much-needed vacation to a tropical paradise. As they lounged on the beach, Sheila's mind wandered back to a time when she almost called it quits.

Early in their relationship, Sheila had been consumed by relationship anxiety, and one of her fixations was Leo's fondness for wearing eccentric hats on vacation. Each time he donned a new one—whether a neon pink flamingo hat or a comically oversized sombrero—she felt a pang of embarrassment, worrying incessantly about what others might think and wondering if Leo was too immature for her.

Leo's resisting Sheila's attempts to stop him from dressing as he'd like caused tension between them and escalated to the point where Sheila was on the brink of walking away. However, now, ten years later, as she sat on the beach watching Leo joyfully belly laugh while adjusting his latest head-turning creation, a wave of gratitude, rather than embarrassment, washed over her. She realized that she had almost let go of a wonderful man over some awful hats.

Sheila recognized how sad it was that she almost let something as trivial as Leo's carefree self-expression tear them apart and how grateful she was she confronted her fears and pushed through her discomfort so that didn't happen. Sure, she still didn't love the hats, but she loved the man wearing them. Sheila realized that leaning into her values and relationship vision rather than her fears ten years ago saved her from missing out on one of the greatest gifts of her life.

SHOULDN'T LOVE BE EASIER?

Sometimes, love feels easy...but a lot of the time, it doesn't. All relationships take work. While they shouldn't feel like hard work *all* the time, healthy, secure partnerships will require conscious and continuous effort. Two individuals being their fullest selves will inevitably experience moments of annoyance or disagreement. Navigating these moments together requires skill—a balance between advocating for yourself and your desires and considering your partner's needs and desires. This balance takes time, effort, and practice to master. You can't be expected to seamlessly create a healthy relationship without practice, role models, and confidence. However, like any new skill, you can practice and improve at it.

There Is Contrast in All We Do

If you never take a risk on a potentially "wrong" partner then you will never know if they're the "right" partner. If you never risk heartbreak, you will never know deep love. If you never risk disappointment, you will never know satisfaction. If you never risk uncertainty, you will never have clarity. There is contrast in all we do, and life happens—and love grows—within and alongside this contrast.

You Are an Expert on You

The skills we've discussed in this book can help guide you toward greater self-trust, confidence, and clarity. They can help you become more relational in your thinking and actions. But they are not a replacement for your inner knowing. You are the expert on you. No one knows what will bring you contentment and fulfillment more than you do. You already possess all that you need within yourself to make a decision, to stick with a decision, and to truly live your life. While external support can certainly be helpful at times, know that you do not need to keep reading books, asking friends, signing up for courses, or taking online quizzes to be sure. It's okay to be unsure and still take the next best step forward.

Live in a Place of Peace

While it doesn't always feel like it, anxiety serves a purpose. It has a place in your life, but that place is not center stage. While you can't completely eliminate feelings of anxiety, you can either choose to live in anxiety and be visited by peace or to live in peace and be visited by anxiety. It's my hope that throughout this book, you've learned how to live more in a place of peace—and you've come to understand that when your anxiety does visit, it's simply bringing you information. It is warning you about potential danger. It is up to you to check in and ask yourself, "Am I really in danger right now? Am I anxious because I'm trying to avoid *future* pain and heartache, or am I feeling pain and heartache *right now?*" Most of the time, your relationship anxiety is focused on protecting you from possibilities in the future, not realities of the present.

Ultimately, all we have is the present. While you certainly would be in good company if you've tried to find one, there is no crystal ball that will tell you if you're going to be bored with your partner, attracted to your partner, betrayed by your partner, or deeply in love with your partner ten years from now. All you have is the knowledge and experiences available to you right now. You can't have certainty, but you can have trust.

Trust Yourself

Trust yourself to make the best decision with the information available to you at this time. Trust that you have the skills, knowledge, and maturity to evolve, personally and relationally. Trust that you are not a passive recipient of a relationship but rather an active co-creator of the relationship you desire. Trust that you will be able to cope if you experience loss, heartache, betrayal, or an unexpected turn in the future. And trust in the possibility of a truly wonderful and satisfying relationship you're excited to commit to.

You are capable and deserving of that loving relationship! Know that you will love, you will laugh, and you will grieve, regardless of which path you take in life. A full life will be packed with sadness and joy, disappointment and surprise, hardships and beauty, doubt and confidence. And you are capable of handling it all!

A FINAL THOUGHT

Regardless of how you're feeling in this very moment, please know that you are not alone. Your relationship anxiety experiences, struggles, and victories are shared by countless others who are walking this path alongside you and by those who have overcome the grip of anxiety and are enjoying fulfilling, imperfect partnerships. You too are capable, resilient, and worthy of love.

So, as you move forward, know that what you need most is not to take another online quiz on love. What you need most may just be to take a value-aligned risk on love. Embrace the journey, embrace the uncertainty, and above all, embrace your ability to take one next best step at a time.

Exercise:
Take a Decision Sabbatical

With relationship anxiety, the pressure to constantly evaluate your relationship can feel overwhelming. As you look ahead toward a future with less anxiety, consider giving yourself a break from the one foot in, one foot out dilemma with a decision sabbatical, a period dedicated to pausing decision-making and evaluation, and simply accept your relationship as it is. This can provide some respite, giving you time and space to pause, rest, and more accurately assess the true success of your relationship.

1. **Commit to the sabbatical:** Decide on a specific duration for your decision sabbatical—perhaps seven days, one month, or even three months. During this period, make a commitment to refrain from making any significant decisions about your relationship. If you're currently in a relationship, remain committed for the chosen time period. If you're single, use this time to stay single and focus on self-care. Note that this does not apply to situations where your physical or emotional safety is threatened. Always remove yourself from unsafe situations as quickly as possible.

2. **Practice acceptance:** During your decision sabbatical, practice accepting your relationship as it is, without judgment or the need to fix anything. Allow yourself to fully experience the ups, downs, and in-betweens without reacting impulsively.

3. **Pause decision-making:** Whether you're feeling disconnected from your partner three days in and are tempted to call it off, or you receive a sweet message from an ex and are considering reconciliation, remember that you've committed to the sabbatical duration.

4. **Reevaluate after the sabbatical:** At the end of your decision sabbatical, reflect on your experience. How did it feel to take a break from decision-making? Did it alleviate pressure from your daily life? Did you experience a sense of freedom with not having to assess the "rightness" of your relationship day-to-day? Did it leave you feeling more connected or disconnected from your partner? Use this reflection to guide any future decisions you may need to make about your relationship.

5. **Trust the process:** Remember that by pausing decision-making and maintaining the status quo for a period of time, you give yourself permission to slow down, zoom out, and be more objective and intentional. Trust that the answers will come in their own time, and in the meantime, focus on nurturing yourself and/or your relationship. Secure and successful relationships are built through experiencing them, not continuously assessing them.

Key Takeaways

- Rather than defining success solely by the duration of a relationship, focus on the quality of the connection, mutual support, and growth, both individually and together. Success encompasses the depth of connection, commitment to shared goals, and creation of a safe space for vulnerability and growth, even if that growth eventually takes you in different directions.

- Relationships are active choices that require commitment, dedication, and risk. Whether staying in a relationship or leaving it, each decision carries its own weight and consequences. Embrace the choice you make and commit fully, whether staying or leaving. A one foot in, one foot out approach will only lead to greater confusion and heartache in the long term.
- Emotional generosity is key to supporting positive dynamics in relationships. It involves giving your partner the benefit of the doubt, voicing concerns compassionately, and appreciating efforts to meet your needs.
- You will learn to cope and move forward, no matter which path you choose and which direction life takes you. Stay focused on your values and vision, and take a risk on love.

RESOURCE LIST

APPS

Calm
https://calm.com

Finch
https://finchcare.com

BOOKS

Anxiously Attached: Becoming More Secure in Life and Love
by Jessica Baum, LMHC

Attached: The New Science of Adult Attachment and How It Can Help You Find—and Keep—Love
by Amir Levine, MD, and Rachel S.F. Heller, MA

Boundaries: When to Say Yes and How to Say No to Take Control of Your Life
by Dr. Henry Cloud and Dr. John Townsend

Dare to Lead: Brave Work. Tough Conversations. Whole Hearts.
by Brené Brown, PhD, MSW

Generation Anxiety: A Millennial and Gen Z Guide to Staying Afloat in an Uncertain World
by Dr. Lauren Cook

I Want This to Work: An Inclusive Guide to Navigating the Most Difficult Relationship Issues We Face in the Modern Age
by Elizabeth Earnshaw, LMFT, CGT

Loving Someone with Anxiety: Understanding & Helping Your Partner
by Kate N. Thieda, MS, LPCA

Relationship OCD: A CBT-Based Guide to Move Beyond Excessive Doubt, Anxiety, and Fear of Commitment in Romantic Relationships
by Sheva Rajaee, MFT

The Four Agreements: A Practical Guide to Personal Freedom
by Don Miguel Ruiz

The Happiness Trap: How to Stop Struggling and Start Living
by Russ Harris

The Mindful Self-Compassion Workbook: A Proven Way to Accept Yourself, Build Inner Strength, and Thrive
by Kristin Neff, PhD, and Christopher Germer, PhD

The Tapping Solution: A Revolutionary System for Stress-Free Living
by Nick Ortner

PODCASTS

The Anxiety Coaches Podcast
https://theanxietycoachespodcast.com

The Anxious Love Coach
https://anxiouslovecoach.com/podcast

The OCD Stories
https://theocdstories.com/episodes

You Love & You Learn
https://youloveandyoulearn.com/podcasts/
you-love-you-learn-podcast

WEBSITES

Anxiety & Depression Association of America
https://adaa.org

Dr. Courtney Paré
https://drcourtneypare.com

Exposure and Response Prevention (ERP) School
https://cbtschool.com/erp-school-lp

International OCD Foundation
https://iocdf.org

National Domestic Violence Hotline
https://thehotline.org

Psychology Today
https://psychologytoday.com/us

Relational Life Institute
https://relationallife.com

Steven C. Hayes, PhD
https://stevenchayes.com

The Gottman Institute
https://gottman.com

INDEX

OVERCOMING RELATIONSHIP ANXIETY

OVERCOMING RELATIONSHIP ANXIETY